The battle for Berlin: end of the Third Reich

The battle for Berlin:

end of the Third Reich

Earl F Ziemke

Pan/Ballantine

Editor-in-Chief: Barrie Pitt
Art Director: Peter Dunbar

Military Consultant: Sir Basil Liddell Hart
Picture Editor: Robert Hunt

Design Assistant: Ann Scott
Cover: Denis Piper
Research Assistant: Yvonne Marsh
Cartographer: Richard Natkiel.Gatrell Ltd

Photographs for this book were especially selected from the following Archives: from left to right page 2-3 Novosti; 9 Search; 12 United Press; 14 Novosti; 16 Imperial War Museum; 19 Sado Opera Mundi; 20 IWM; 23 Novosti; 28 Novosti; 29 Keystone Press; 30-31 Novosti; 35 Keystone; 37 Ullstein; 39 Ullstein; 40-41 Novosti; 44 Novosti; 46 Bibliothek fur Zeitgeschichte; 47 IWM; 48 Bibliothek fur Zeitgeschichte; 52 Novosti; 53 US Army; 57 US Army; 62 IWM; 63 US Army; 72 Suddeutscher Verlag; 73 Ullstein; 77 Ullstein; 81 Novosti; 82-83 IWM; 86 Ullstein; 87 Ullstein; 89 Ullstein; 90 Ullstein; 91 Ullstein; 96-97 Ullstein; 98 Sudd. Verlag; 99 Ullstein; 100-101 Ullstein; 102 Ullstein; 103 Ullstein; 104-105 Ullstein; 106 Ullstein; 107 Associated Press; 108 Ullstein; 109 Ullstein; 112-113 Ullstein; 114-115 Sudd. Verlag; 116 Ullstein; 117 Novosti/ Ullstein; 119 Sudd. Verlag; 122 Ullstein; 123 Sudd. Verlag; 124 Sudd. Verlag; 125 Ullstein; 126 Bibliothek fur Zeitgeschichte; 127 Ullstein; 128 Bibliothek fur Zeitgeschichte; 129 IWM; 130 Novosti; 131 Novosti; 132 Ullstein; 133 Novosti; 134 Sudd. Verlag; 135 Ullstein; 137 Sudd. Verlag; 138 Associated Press; 139 Ullstein; 140 Ullstein; 141 Popperfoto; 142 Ullstein; 143 Ullstein; 146-147 Ullstein; 148 Ullstein; 149 Ullstein, 150-151 Ullstein; 152 IWM; 153 IWM; 154 Ullstein; 155 Ullstein; 156 IWM; 157 Sado Opera Mundi; 158-159 Sudd. Verlag; 160 Bibliothek fur Zeitgeschichte.

Copyright © Earl F Ziemke 1968

ISBN 0 330 24007 2

First published in the United States 1968
This Pan/Ballantine edition published 1974 by
Pan Books Ltd, 33 Tothill Street, London SW1

Printed in Great Britain by
Butler and Tanner Ltd, Frome and London

Contents

Cold war city

Introduction by Barrie Pitt

No city in modern history has borne more eloquent testimony to the tenuous nature of warlike alliances than Berlin.

At the moment when the American Chiefs-of-Staff began to concentrate on a military victory to the war in Europe, and ignore the political consequences of its outcome, the seeds were sown for a conflict of potentially greater moment than the one which was even then coming to an end.

To the extent that he was a military commander, charged with securing a victory over the enemy's armed forces, Eisenhower was perfectly justified in halting his drive at the Elbe line. Whether Truman, as the statesman ultimately responsible, was right in endorsing the military view is a another matter. Yet he too was powerless to alter the course of events, since the decision was that of his recently dead predecessor, and at that stage would bear no fundamental alteration.

So the fault, if fault there is, can be traced back to Roosevelt. He, trusting Stalin's good intentions almost to the point of naivety, and maintaining with blythe self-confidence that he could 'handle' Stalin, was filled with idealistic enthusiasm for a post-war *entente* which would create a paradise on earth. Roosevelt therefore went all out to capture the fanciful dream of a military victory untarnished by post-war political considerations.

So Stalin was taken at face value, and instead of a liberated Eastern Europe, its people free from the Nazi tyranny, there is today an Eastern Europe burdened by the yoke of a different, possibly greater tyranny, as is illustrated by the bloody experience of Budapest, the almost bloodless but no less bitter recent events in Prague, and above all Berlin, the ludicrous anomaly of a city artificially divided, one part desperately trying to preserve its integrity miles from the boundary where its political, spiritual, cultural and economic connexions abruptly end. With the communist blockade of the city, the airlift, and most recently the wall, Berlin has stood, since the brief elated meeting of the Allied soldiers was terminated by the iron curtain's clanging descent, as the focal point of the cold war, the epitome of man's inability to establish governments which can operate in a spirit of mutual trust.

Sir Basil Liddell Hart, the military consultant to these volumes, foresaw the danger as early as 1941, when in his book 'The Strategy of Indirect Approach' he wrote with prophetic accuracy:

'If you concentrate exclusively on victory, with no thought for the after effect, you may be too exhausted to profit by the peace, while it is almost certain that the peace will be a bad one, containing the germs of another war. This is a lesson supported by abundant experience. The risks become greater still in any war that is waged by a coalition, for in such a case a too complete victory inevitably complicates the problem of making a just and wise peace settlement. Where there is no longer the counter-balance of an opposing force to control the appetites of the victors, there is no check on the conflict of views and interests between the parties to the alliance. The divergence is then apt to become so acute as to turn the comradeship of common danger into the hostility of mutual dissatisfaction – so that the ally of one war becomes the enemy in the next.'

Yet war and its consequences are fraught with paradox, and it may be that the decision by the Americans to leave Berlin to the Red Army has served Europe, western Europe at least, better than we generally realise. Is it not true, perhaps, that if the loose ends of the war had been more neatly tied up, the United States might have returned to a policy of isolationism, and declined to become involved in post-war European politics? Would the near bankrupt British and French then have been able to resist the might of an increasingly powerful USSR, motivated by Stalinist aims? After all, the American presence in Europe, almost a voluntary penance for failing to achieve a satisfactory political outcome, has at least served for over twenty years to keep the cold war more or less cold.

But that is speculation, and in concentrating on the broad political picture, one is apt to forget that Berlin, like any other city, is primarily a collection of people. And it was the people who suffered most in Berlin's eventual fall. Earl Ziemke's book has the great merit of tackling the subject from both important angles – the military and the personal. In dispassionate detail he traces the course of events that led to the battle in the city, while at the same time his book succeeds in capturing, graphically and memorably, the atmosphere as the Russians closed in. At a distance of twenty years in time, one can hear still the screams of soldiers and civilians, women and children, as the Red Army fought into the heart of the city, bent on extracting the full vengeful price for the indignities suffered on Russian soil at German hands. Finally this horror gives way to tragi-comedy, as the Allies, even at their moment of victory, find themselves unable to agree on how the peace should be organised, and how the occupied territories should be apportioned.

And at the centre of the book stands the dominating figure of Adolph Hitler, decrepit now and war-worn, but determined to fight on, as he said, 'until five-past-midnight'. He refused to surrender or leave, rejected the advice of his own generals, and waited for the miracle that would save his empire. His is the picture, all too familiar in the world of second rate films, of the maniac dictator screaming defiance and blaming all and sundry as the walls of his castle crumble around him.

Were it not for the memory of millions of Jews, untold war casualties and the inestimable waste of material resources and human effort, all of which can be laid directly at Hitler's door, it might almost be funny.

The story of the fall of Berlin, the climax to six years of the greatest conflict in human history, is a story on the grand scale. Earl Ziemke's book more than does it justice.

Beyond the horizon

Buried deep in the evergreen forest twenty-five miles east of Rastenburg, East Prussia, the *Wolfsschanze* (Wolf's Lair) was, more than Berlin, the nerve centre of Germany in the Second World War. There, in 1941, Hitler had established the Führer Headquarters for the predicted two to two and a half months' campaign against the Soviet Union. There, usually at about noon and midnight, he received the twice-daily reports of the service commands, and from there he issued his orders by telephone and teletype. With him in a closely guarded compound he kept only the Chief of the Armed Forces High Command (OKW), Field-Marshal Wilhelm Keitel; the Chief of the Operations Staff, OKW, Colonel-General Alfred Jodl, and his staff; liaison officers from each of the services; and a small political staff. Hitler's visits to the Reich capital after June 1941, and until January 1945 were rare and brief. Officials who needed to see him made the trip to the *Wolfsschanze* either by air or on the daily courier trains from Berlin. In addition to his functions as Chancellor and Commander-in-Chief of the German Armed Forces, Hitler had, in late 1941, assumed the post of Commander-in-Chief, Army. The Army High Command (OKH), respon-sible under Hitler for operations on the Eastern Front, was established just outside Rastenburg, twenty minutes away from the *Wolfsschanze* by rail.

On the morning 14th June 1944, at Rastenburg, the Chief-of-Staff Army, Colonel-General Kurt Zeitzler, spoke to the assembled chiefs of staff of all the army groups and armies on the Eastern Front. The war in Russia was entering its fourth summer; and he and Hitler had reached a conclusion as to what was to be expected during the coming months. To the chiefs-of-staff representing Army Group Centre, Zeitzler half apologised for having brought them on an unnecessary trip. What he had to say, he told them, would not 'particularly concern Army Group Centre'. The Soviet summer offensive would strike in the south, toward the Balkans. The Russians, he predicted, were not ready yet to take the direct route into Germany. He was wrong.

The Russians had waited through April and May and the first weeks of June 1944. At Tehran, in December 1943, President Franklin D Roosevelt and Prime Minister Winston S Churchill had promised them a full-scale second front in the spring of 1944. The promise was kept on 6th June

Hitler and his essential maps, in consultation with Generals von Rundstedt, and, left Keitel

with the landing in Normandy. In the meantime, Marshals of the Soviet Union Georgi K Zhukov and Aleksander M Vasilevsky had nearly completed the most massive Soviet build-up of the war thus far – not on the south flank, as Zeitzler predicted, but against Army Group Centre. In the first three weeks of June alone they brought in 75,000 railroad carloads of troops, supplies, and ammunition. Together the Russians had 1,200,000 men to throw against Army Group Centre's 700,000. Farther back, the Soviet Supreme Command, the *Stavka*, held again as many troops in reserve to nourish the battle.

For three years Army Group Centre had been the bulwark of the German Eastern Front. In 1941 it had made the drive on Moscow. Since then, as its neighbours on the north and south were driven back, it had retreated but never as disastrously as the southern army groups had from Stalingrad and the Caucasus or as Army Group North had from Leningrad. In June 1944, Army Group Centre still held the

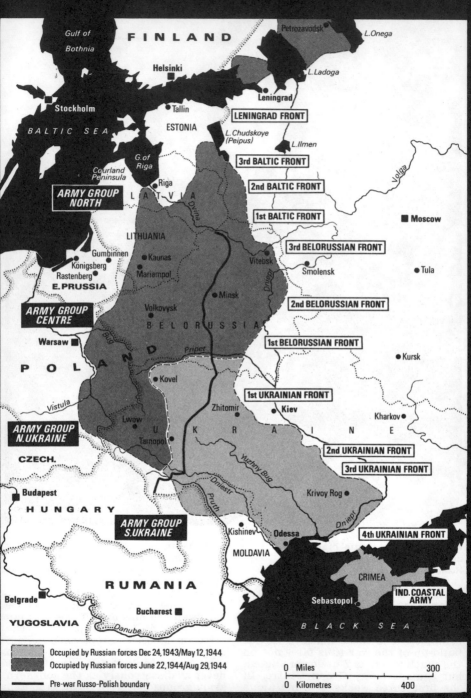

FINLAND

Gulf of Bothnia

Helsinki

L.Onega

Petrozavodsk

L.Ladoga

Stockholm

Leningrad

BALTIC SEA

Tallin

LENINGRAD FRONT

ESTONIA

L.Chudskoye (Peipus)

L.Ilmen

3rd BALTIC FRONT

Volga

G. of Riga

Courland Peninsula

Riga

2nd BALTIC FRONT

L A T V I A

Dvina

1st BALTIC FRONT

ARMY GROUP NORTH

LITHUANIA

Moscow

Kaunas

3rd BELORUSSIAN FRONT

Mariampol

Gumbinnen

Vitebsk

Konigsberg

Smolensk

Tula

Rastenberg

Minsk

E.PRUSSIA

Volkovysk

Dniepr

2nd BELORUSSIAN FRONT

ARMY GROUP CENTRE

B E L O R U S S I A

Bug

Warsaw

Pripet

1st BELORUSSIAN FRONT

P O L A N D

Kursk

Kovel

1st UKRAINIAN FRONT

Vistula

Zhitomir

Kiev

Lwow

U K R A I N E

Kharkov

ARMY GROUP N.UKRAINE

Tarnopol

Yuzhny Bug

2nd UKRAINIAN FRONT

CZECH.

3rd UKRAINIAN FRONT

Dniestr

Krivoy Rog

Budapest

Prut

Dniepr

HUNGARY

ARMY GROUP S.UKRAINE

Kishinev

Odessa

4th UKRAINIAN FRONT

MOLDAVIA

CRIMEA

IND. COASTAL ARMY

R U M A N I A

Sebastopol

Belgrade

Bucharest

B L A C K   S E A

YUGOSLAVIA

Danube

Occupied by Russian forces Dec 24,1943/May 12,1944

Occupied by Russian forces June 22,1944/Aug 29,1944

Pre-war Russo-Polish boundary

| 0 | Miles | 300 |
| 0 | Kilometres | 400 |

The Germans lose their last footholds in Russia ; the battle for Poland begins

historic Vitebsk 'Gate', the gap between the headwaters of the Dvina and Dniepr rivers that opened toward Moscow 300 miles away. Behind the army group lay Minsk, capital of the Soviet Belorussian Republic, Warsaw, and Berlin.

The difference in the distances which the American and British armies had to cover from the Cotentin Peninsula in France and the Russian armies from the Vitebsk Gate to Berlin was less than one hundred miles, somewhat more than six hundred and fifty miles for the former and somewhat less than seven hundred and fifty for the latter. Strategically the threats to Germany were about equal. In the East the great land buffer the Germans had acquired in the 1941 and 1942 campaigns had become badly eroded; in the West the English Channel, a barrier Hitler had not ventured to cross in his best days, had become a broad highway carrying the men and weapons of his enemies. Unable to convince himself that the main landing would not come at the Pas-de-Calais, Hitler had failed to send his reserves against the Normandy landing. With a fine, if wholly unintentional, impartiality, he had also taken away a third of Army Group Centre's heavy artillery, half of its tank destroyers, and 88% of its tanks so that he might be ready to meet the expected Soviet thrust in the south.

On the morning of 22nd June 1944, the third anniversary of the German invasion, Zhukov and Vasilevsky launched their armies against Army Group Centre. The army group commander, Field-Marshal Ernst Busch, was away at the Führer Headquarters awaiting an interview with Hitler which he hoped would result in getting some of his tanks and guns returned. It was too late. The Russians showed elegance in their tactical conceptions, economy of effort, and control that did not fall short of the Germans' own performance in the early war years. They used tightly concentrated infantry and artillery to breach the front on narrow sectors. Their tanks stayed out of sight until an opening was ready, then went straight through without bothering about the flanks. It was their best performance of the war to date and

better than some that were to follow. In twelve days Army Group Centre lost twenty-five of its forty-three divisions.

In three and a half weeks the Russians reconquered Belorussia and all but destroyed Army Group Centre. On 17th July from dawn until after dark, they marched 57,000 German prisoners, ten and twelve abreast, through the main streets of Moscow to mark the victory. The next day at Führer Headquarters, Zeitzler and Field-Marshal Walter Model, who had replaced Busch in command of Army Group Centre, attempted to persuade Hitler to take Army Group North out of the Baltic States, where it was in imminent danger of being cut off anyway, and use its divisions to rebuild Army Group Centre. Hitler refused, Zeitzler offered his resignation, and when Hitler refused that too, reported himself sick.

In France, on 18th July, the Americans captured St Lô. The Russians had covered up to two hundred miles in June and July. The United States 1st Army and British 2nd Army under General Sir Bernard L Montgomery had covered at the most twenty miles; but at St Lô they were almost out of the murderous hedgerows of the Normandy *bocage*, the earth and hedge-walled fields that could not be traversed even by tanks unless they were equipped with bulldozer blades. The Allied Supreme Commander, General Dwight D Eisenhower, had over a million men and a half million tons of supplies ashore in the beachhead by then. The British and American air forces had absolute command of the air, and the Germans scarcely dared show themselves in the open on the roads in daylight. Field-Marshal Günther von Kluge, who replaced Field-Marshal Erwin Rommel after Rommel was injured on the 17th when his car was strafed by Allied planes, could neither contemplate driving the Allied armies off the beaches nor prevent for very long a breakout into the interior of France.

German strategy was bankrupt. No one realised that better than the officers of the Army General Staff and the army and army group commands. They knew too that while Hitler lived peace – short of the peace brought

11

Hitler escapes assasination; shaken and huddled under a cloak, he returns to the scene with Himmler at his side. Mussolini and Göring are behind

by total destruction – was impossible. A half hour after noon on 20th July 1944, at the *Wolfsschanze*, Colonel Count Klaus Schenk von Stauffenberg, a general staff officer, entered the room in which Hitler was holding a customary noon situation conference, placed a briefcase under the long oak table at which Hitler was seated, and walked out. From a distance, Stauffenberg watched as, a dozen minutes later, a blast which he described with a combat officer's experienced eye as the equivalent of an impacting 150 mm artillery shell blew out the walls of the building he had just left. The bomb he had planted in the briefcase next to Hitler's feet had done its work, and Stauffenberg hurried to the airport thinking that by the time he completed the three-hour flight to Berlin his fellow conspirators

in the Army would have the most dangerous element of the Nazi apparatus, the SS, under control. That the third Reich would then quickly come to an end seemed a certainty, since some of the most highly placed officers – among them Field-Marshals Rommel and Kluge – while not active in the conspiracy, had promised their support once Hitler was dead.

But Hitler was not dead. The bomb injured nineteen officers in the room with him, three of them fatally; and it demolished the building; but Hitler escaped with relatively minor burns, bruises, and a burst ear drum. Some days after the explosion had stopped a bothersome tremor he had had in his left leg. He added that he would not recommend the treatment to anyone else, however. To Hitler, and doubtless to many others in Germany, the escape appeared to be nothing less than the work of Providence. If the conference had not been held that day in one of the few wooden structures still standing in the *Wolfsschanze* but in the reinforced concrete bunker where it was usually held, the force of the explosion would have been so intensified that he could not have escaped.

Hitler did not die on the 20th July, but Germany's last chance of finding a rational way out of the war did. The army *coup* collapsed within hours, and in the succeeding weeks the Gestapo rooted out every detectable trace of resistance. Kluge committed suicide. Hitler gave Rommel the choice of doing the same or facing trial and the more ghastly death being reserved for the convicted conspirators. The army, in a fit of panic, waived its cherished right to try its own members, expelled the accused from its ranks, and turned them over to the Nazi People's Court. From there most passed into the hands of SS executioners. Colonel-General Heinz Guderian, who replaced Zeitzler as Army Chief of Staff, ordered all officers to display an 'exemplary [Nazi] attitude on political affairs and that publically.' Zeitzler had not been in the plot, but it had taken place in his staff, which was enough. To make certain the army could not turn against him in the future, Hitler gave command of the Replacement Army to the Reichsführer-SS, Heinrich Himmler. The Replacement Army controlled all troops stationed in Germany.

During the last day of July, Soviet tanks closed to the Vistula river within sight of Warsaw. South of the city, the Soviet 8th Guards Army and 1st Tank Army were already ferrying troops and tanks across the river into bridgeheads on the west bank. On the north, the German III Panzer Army's front broke open between Kaunas and Mariampol, offering the Russians a clear path to the border of East Prussia twenty miles away. The army commander, Colonel-General Hans Reinhardt, moved his headquarters behind the border and discovered with horror that, on Hitler's orders, nothing had been done about evacuating the civilians, even the women and children. Between the flanks of Army Group Centre and Army Group North, a Soviet guards mechanised corps drove to the Gulf of Riga west of Riga and broke Army Group North's

contact by land with the main front. That day, too, something else happened: for the first time in six weeks the Soviet offensive faltered. The Russians did not expand their handhold on the Baltic coast. Colonel-General I D Chernyakovsky, Reinhardt's opponent, ignored the opening between Mariampol and Kaunas. The tanks attacking toward Warsaw, apparently running short of fuel, suddenly slowed almost to a stop.

Although United States 1st Army troops breaking out of the Cotentin Peninsula had passed Avranches during the day, to Hitler, reviewing the situation at midnight on the 31st, the danger in the East still appeared the greater. The loss of ground, he said, was not entirely bad; it shortened his lines of communications; but the psychological effects on his allies, Finland, Rumania, and Hungary, not to mention Germany itself, would be severe if the Russians managed to carry the war to German soil in East Prussia or Upper Silesia. He blamed everything on the defeatism in the General Staff as evidenced by the 20th July plot. Nevertheless, he had stabilised the Eastern Front in as bad situations before, and he predicted he would do it again. For the last time he was right.

August was the Western Allies' month. Turning east out of Normandy and Brittany, they cleared a massive blunt wedge of ground between the Seine and the Loire in two weeks. Paris fell on the 25th. In the meantime the United States 7th Army and French 1st Army had landed at St Tropez and Marseilles on the Mediterranian coast and begun pushing north along the Rhône-Saône Valley. On the day they took Paris, Eisenhower's main forces, 21st Army Group under Montgomery – now exclusively British – and United States 12th Army Group under General Omar Bradley, the British on the left and the Americans on the right, turned north and began driving toward the German border. In two weeks they would be joined on the far right, north of the Swiss border, by the Mediterranean invasion force, which would then become 6th Army Group.

For the Western Allies victory suddenly seemed close in August only to fade into the distance just as suddenly in September. Hitler's bid to frighten England out of the war failed as Montgomery's troops overran the V-1 rocket launching sites in north-western France and Belgium. On 11th September American spearhead troops crossed out of Luxembourg into Germany. But by then Eisenhower's armies were outrunning their supplies. General George S Patton's United States 3rd Army had already been stopped for nearly a week by lack of fuel. The same was threatening the other armies. Supplies were arriving at the Continent, but getting them to the front over war-wracked roads and railroads was another matter. Montgomery urged putting all the available resources into a single-pronged thrust by his army group across Holland and North Germany to Berlin. Eisenhower refused. He would not risk sending one army group on a 350-mile hussar's ride, particularly when to do it meant immobilising all the rest of his forces. The pursuit was over. Montgomery learned that before the end of the month when he lost an attempt to open a corridor to the Rhine south of Arnhem. The Americans discovered it too when they attempted to advance to the Rhine via Aachen and had – after most of three weeks spent in house-to-house fighting–to be content with the lesser satisfaction of having secured the first German city to surrender in the Second World War.

In the East, by October, Finland, Rumania, and Bulgaria had surrender-

ed. North of the Arctic Circle, German XX Mountain Army was retreating out of Finland. On north flank of the main front, Army Group North was trapped on the Courland Peninsula. On the south flank, Soviet armies were closing to the Yugoslav border and beginning a drive toward Budapest. When three Soviet armies charged across the East Prussian border on 16th October, headed toward Gumbinnen, Hitler gave up his last attempt to regain contact by land with Army Group North, used the troops to defend Gumbinnen, and thereby saved himself the embarrassment of simultaneously losing cities in both the East and the West. After that the battles subsided on the Eastern Front north of the Carpathians. The Russians, too, had been having supply trouble since September.

In the summer offensives the Russians and the Western Allies had both covered more than half their original distances to Berlin. From Aachen and from Warsaw they now had identical distances, 325 miles, still to go. For both, Berlin was still a remote objective. Eisenhower's attention centred on the Ruhr, which was closer and – to his mind – strategically more important. The Russians, after taking bridgeheads upstream and downstream on the Vistula, had stayed on the right bank opposite Warsaw through September and watched the Germans destroy the *Armia Krajowa* (Polish Home Army) in the city. In the Autumn they seemed more intent on Budapest and Belgrade than on the German capital.

Soviet infantrymen advance

Shifting tides

A prudent German government would have used the pause at the end of summer 1944 to seek an armistice and so escape the final wave of destruction. The Allies more than half expected even Hitler's government to do that. They were mistaken. Hitler would not consider – and after 20th July nobody else in Germany dared to consider – ending the war on the only terms then being offered:– unconditional surrender. While Hitler lived, Germany would go on fighting; the strength it had left was not enough to affect the outcome but was enough to prolong the agony.

The German army, for the moment holding its own in the field, was burning out at the core. Between June and November the total irrecoverable losses amounted to 1,400,000 men. On the Eastern Front the German strength in November was 400,000 men less than in June and 700,000 less than in January 1944. Hitler resorted to organisational and mathematical sleight of hand. He created new infantry divisions and Panzer brigades by using the replacements that should have gone to existing units. He authorised artillery corps with brigade strengths and Panzer brigades of two battalions or even one battalion. Himmler, as Commanding General, Replacement Army, reported 1,500,000 men available for call-up; but of these, nearly a million could not possibly reach the field until 1945, if then. In the meantime, the divisons at the front had over 800,000 unfilled authorised spaces – after a 700,000 space reduction in the 1944 tables of organisation.

The German war economy was becoming a scene of wild contrasts. The aircraft plants turned out 3,000 fighters in September 1944, a record for the war. In the same month all of the synthetic petrol plants were bombed out of operation. During June 1944, the Luftwaffe had consumed 90,000,000 gallons of avaiation fuel; its entire supply for the rest of the war amounted to no more than 95,000,000 gallons. Armoured vehicle production, including tanks, assault-guns, and self-propelled artillery, reached its wartime peak – 1,854 units – in December 1944. By then, however, the blast furnaces and rolling mills of the Ruhr were producing only about half as much iron and steel as they had in September 1944 and about a third of their January 1944 output. In October the automotive plants turned out 12,000 trucks by rebuilding all the disabled army trucks to be found in Germany. In December truck production fell to 3,000 units. The shortage of motor fuel was as stringent as that of aviation fuel, and by the end of the year Hitler planned to mount his Panzer Grenadiers on bicycles, consoling himself with the thought that trucks created traffic jams.

On the Allied side, disappointment at August or September's not having brought the end of the war could not affect the conviction that Germany was beaten. While the armies set about preparing blows that it seemed could hardly fail again to convince the Germans, the governments looked ahead to the time after the surrender. In London, on 12th September 1944, the United States, Great Britain, and the Soviet Union signed a *Protocol on Zones of Occupation and Administration of the 'Greater Berlin' Area.* Two months later, on 14th November, they completed an *Agreement on Control Machinery in Germany.* Those two documents for the first time gave tangible form and purpose to Allied operations beyond the strictly military objective of defeating the German armies in the field. Incidentally, but nonetheless inevitably, they made Berlin – until then a convenient reference point or at most a desirable prize – the ultimate political focal point of the Allied war effort.

That Germany would be occupied, not partially as in the First World War but completely, had been perhaps the one undisputed Allied assumption of the war. What had long remained unsettled was the question as to how the occupation would be accomplished.

Advance from the west. British soldiers build a prefabricated port in Normandy

Lieutenant-General Sir F E Morgan had considered the problem in the summer of 1943 when, as Chief-of-Staff to the Supreme Allied Commander (COSSAC), he began the planning for the Normandy invasion. It had then seemed possible, even likely, that Germany would collapse before the British and Americans reached the Continent, in which case the Russians might occupy the greater part if not all of Germany. Consequently, United States Secretary of State Cordell Hull and British Foreign Minister Anthony Eden were pleased, on visiting Moscow in October 1943, to find the Russians willing to discuss a tripartite arrangement for the postwar treatment of Germany. By then the Western Allies also had something more than pious intentions on which to found their claim to a part in the German occupation. At the Big Three meeting scheduled for Tehran in December, President Franklin D Roosevelt and Prime Minister Winston S Churchill intended to give Marshal Joseph V Stalin a solid commitment for opening a second front in Europe in the spring of 1945. Anticipating that, Soviet Foreign Minister Vyacheslav M Molotov agreed on behalf of his government to join in establishing a high-level negotiating body, the European Advisory Commission (EAC), to make agreements pertaining to the occupation for the three governments.

The EAC, with Sir William Strang representing Great Britain and Ambassadors Fedor T Gousev and John G Winant the Soviet Union and the United States, had begun its work in London in January 1944. Settling the first item on its agenda, a surrender document for Germany, took five months (from January to June). The British and Americans fell to arguing over the text; and the Russians were perfectly content not to move on to the next items, occupation zones and the control machinery.

After the Normandy landing in June, everyone's interest in the second and third items increased. By late August, when Eisenhower's armies were racing toward the German border, the Russians became impatient to get the agreements drafted and signèd. They then presented a proposal on the control machinery so finely calculated to reconcile divergent United States and British views that both accepted it practically without argument.

The protocol on zones signed in September divided Germany into an eastern zone and two western zones. The eastern zone, then still including East Prussia, could not logically have gone anywhere but to the Soviet Union, and Berlin lay deep within it. Berlin had been a problem all along, but the governments had been unable to suggest any other drawing of the boundaries that would not have both greatly reduced the Soviet zone or grossly mangled the German internal administrative boundaries. The protocol described 'Great Berlin,' that is, *Gross Berlin* as established by German law in 1920, as a 'special area.' It would be occupied by the forces of the three powers, each in a separate sector, but would be administered jointly. How the British and American forces would get to and from their Berlin sectors across the intervening Soviet territory was not mentioned, though it could be, and in fact was assumed, that the existence of the Western sectors implied rights of access to them.

Two months later, the agreement on control machinery committed the three governments to set up jointly two administrative bodies in occupied Germany; a city administration for Berlin designated as the *Komandatura,* and a Control Council. The *Komandatura,* headed by the three Berlin sector commandants, would function under supervision of the Control Council, which would also make decisions affecting Germany as a whole and control the German central administration. The commanders-in-chief of the three zones would head the Control Council. Although the agreement did not specifically say so, the mission of supervising the German central authorities made Berlin the logical seat for the Control Council.

With the signing of the zones protocol and the agreement on control machinery, the most pressing questions related to the ending of the war appeared to be settled, except for one – how to accomplish the final German defeat. On the Eastern Front, between the Carpathians and the Baltic, the Russians were stocking up for another winter offensive. The Western Allies after having had victory almost in their grasp, were reluctant to see the war prolonged into the new year. Toward the end of October, the United States Chief-of-Staff, General of the Army George C Marshall, proposed to release hitherto restricted secret weapons, including the proximity fuse, and to draw on the strategic reserves for an all-out effort to bring Germany down by 1st January 1945. The British Chiefs-of-Staff backed Montgomery's contention that the weight ought to be on the north flank, on the most direct approaches to the Ruhr and Berlin, even if that meant neglecting other lines of thrust. The obstacle frustrating all plans for a fast drive into Germany was the state of Allied supplies. The great Belgian port of Antwerp, fully capable of handling the tonnages needed by Eisenhower's armies, had been in Allied hands since 4th September, but the Scheldt Estuary, its connection to the sea, was not cleared of Germans until 8th November, and the first convoy could not begin unloading at Antwerp until the end of the month. Eisenhower declined to make another big move until his supply troubles were resolved and he could develop thrusts both in the north and the south.

Nevertheless, the feeling that victory was near remained strong. The British Joint Planning Staff, while expressing doubts about Marshall's hoped-for date of 1st January 1945, considered 31st January as not unreasonable and expected the war's end by 15th May at the latest. The Supreme Headquarters Allied Expeditionary Forces (SHAEF), Eisenhower's staff for command of military operations against Germany, was already having to protect its interest in the initial phase of the occupation against the burgeoning Control Council staffs. In anticipation of the EAC agreements, the British had begun forming their element of the Control Council in June 1944, the Americans theirs in August. In the Autumn the Control Council elements negotiated agreements, only half-whimsically named the Treaties of Versailles and St Cyr, with SHAEF. SHAEF retained control of military government in Germany while hostilities lasted and for an indefinite but brief period thereafter. On the other hand, SHAEF agreed to adjust the policies it intended to initiate to the plans being worked out by the Control Council elements. By late fall SHAEF had the premier United States military government detachment, Detachment A1A1, training in Belgium for a mission in Berlin; and the United States and British elements of the Control had Advanced Ministerial Control Parties standing by ready to move to Berlin with the first SHAEF forces to take control of the German ministries. When the Russian element of the Control Council reached London, as the British and Americans expected, the Allied administration would be complete and capable of descending on Berlin, organised and functioning. The Russians never came.

At conferences in early December, Eisenhower and Montgomery agreed that the main effort of the next all-out offensive, expected now to begin during the early weeks of 1945, would be on the north. Eisenhower intended also to develop a southern thrust, but only to the extent that he could do so without impairing the thrust in the north. The two would be separated south of Aachen by the seventy mile wide band of the Ardennes Forest. Before the main offensive began the armies north and south of the Ardennes would undertake to push their lines east to the Rhine. In the first weeks of December they were already probing some of the likely approaches. Several small, sharp battles dotted the front north and south of the Ardennes. In the centre, thinly manned, the Ardennes front was quiet. It did not figure in the projected offensive.

Winter comes early in the Ardennes. Rain and snow alternate from the middle of November to the middle of December, tapering off thereafter into sleet, snow and cold. Clouds brush the tops of the evergreen forest and send swirls of mist and fog down to the ground beneath. Then the Eifel, the German extension of the Ardennes. can hide an army or two or three with all their troops, artillery, tanks, and supplies. Hitler knew that. He also remembered 1940 when, after part of the original Plan 'Yellow' for the campaign against France had fallen into Allied hands, he had been forced to find a way of regaining surprise and had decided to launch his main thrust through the Ardennes, until then considered impassable by mechanised armies even in good weather. The result had been the *Sichelschnitt*, the scythe stroke, the drive through the Ardennes and the hook to the right that in a bare two weeks had thrown the British back to the beaches at Dunkirk and completely unhinged the Maginot Line. When the generals protested that the Army could not do in 1944 what it had done in 1940, Hitler remembered that they had protested and been wrong in 1940 too.

In the first two weeks of December three armies, VI SS Panzer, V Panzer, and VII Army, moved into the Eifel and its fringes south-east of Aachen and north-east of Trier. Into them

German troops march to counterattack in the east

Hitler put 28 divisions, half of his entire strength on the Western front. More than 1,400 tanks and self-propelled assault-guns, almost as many as were then on the whole Eastern Front, were to lead the attack. To keep the armies rolling, Hitler earmarked 70% of the December truck production for the offensive. The Luftwaffe could only promise a thousand planes and would probably be too pinched for fuel to put up that many: but Hitler expected the weather to help by keeping the Allies from exploiting their vast air superiority. On the night of 13th December and the three succeeding nights, in darkness, rain, and fog and under the cover of the forest, the German troops marched the last fifty miles to their line of departure.

The six American divisions holding the United States 1st Army's front in the Ardennes were so much surprised when artillery and rocket fire crashed in on them on the morning of 16th December that the surprise, for the

The Ardennes offensive; German soldiers advance

moment, lost its effect. On the first day they stood off the waves of German infantry coming at them out of the woods believing that the Germans were staging local attacks for obscure and possibly inconsequential purposes of their own. Allied Intelligence had completely failed to detect the German build-up, partly because of the weather but mostly because it had ceased to believe that the Germans had that much bite left in them.

In the next eight days the plans for and early advance to and across the Rhine evaporated in a nightmare of uncertainty. Eisenhower's northern and southern attack forces. Montgomery's 21st Army Group and Bradley's 12th Army Group, regrouped in haste to blunt the enemy wedge being driven between their flanks. The

Germans fought with a ruthlessness they had not yet displayed on the Western Front. The VIth SS Panzer Army, in particular, showed small mercy either to civilians or to American soldiers who fell into its hands. Had Eisenhower's north and south corner posts, St Vith and Bastogne, not held – St Vith until 23rd December and Bastogne, although encircled, throughout the battle – the Allied condition could have been much more serious. As it was, one German spearhead reached Celles, three miles east of the Meuse river and eighty miles west of its line of departure, on 23rd December. The next day, for the first time in the battle, the weather cleared, and the Allied air forces at once brought their enormous weight to bear. After Christmas Day the issue was no longer much in doubt, but weeks of the hardest fighting lay ahead.

Build-up in the east

General Guderian, the Chief of the German General Staff, spent Christmas Eve at the *Adlehorst*, the Führer Headquarters in the Taunus Mountains ten miles north-west of Bad Nauheim. Hitler had left Rastenburg early in December and after a short stay in Berlin had moved to the *Adlehorst* before the Ardennes offensive began. From there he had also directed the victorious 1940 campaign in the West. Guderian had arrived that morning after an overnight trip in his command train from the Army headquarters and communications centre at the *Maybachlager* in Zossen, twenty miles south of Berlin. He had come to ask Hitler to call off the offensive in the Ardennes and send the excess divisions east. The attack in the West, in the sober judgement of the General Staff, was now destined to fail and ought to be called off, particularly since the Russians, meanwhile, had completed their biggest build-up of the war on the Eastern Front north of the Carpathians.

Hitler refused to abandon the Ardennes operation and scoffed at Guderian's figure on the strength of Soviet forces deployed along the Vistula River and the East Prussian border. The Russians, he said, were trying to pass off the 'Greatest bluff since Genghis Khan.' He would not consider creating reserves by taking troops from the West, from Norway, or from Courland; the Eastern Front would have to shift for itself. At dinner that night, Himmler, a policeman lately embarked on a new career as an army group commander in Alsace, advised Guderian not to worry so much. The Russians, he insisted, would not attack. They were trying a 'gigantic fraud'. For the habitués of the *Adlehorst* the Eastern Front seemed to be too far away to worry about.

For Germany, in the waning days of 1944, the end did not in fact seem as near either in the East or the West as it had just a few months earlier. The jaws of the vice in which the Western Allies and the Soviet Union had undertaken to squeeze out the last German resistance were not closing. The Ardennes offensive, it could be seen, was not going to be a blow that would restore Germany's strategic freedom of action; but the Germans had the initiative and it would be a while before the Western Allies could resume their march toward the heart of the Reich. North of the Carpathians the Russians had not made a substantial advance in two and a half months. In Hungary Soviet armies surrounded

21

Budapest on Christmas Day, but the forces west of the city were so nearly in balance that a relief did not appear impossible. The German occupation troops were evacuating Greece, Albania, and southern Yugoslavia but doing so under control and without haste. In Italy, German Army Group C had stopped the British and Americans at the Gothic Line.

Nevertheless, Hitler was militarily bankrupt. He had invested all the effort he and the troops were capable of in the Ardennes, and it was not enough. Henceforth, he could only fight for time. and he knew it. At the end of December he told one of the generals, 'The war will not last as long as it has lasted. That is absolutely certain. Nobody can endure it; we cannot and the others cannot. The question is, who will endure longer? It must be he who has everything at stake. We have everything at stake.' General Erich Ludendorff had preached endurance in almost identical terms during the last months of the First World War – until his own nerves failed him.

Hitler's nerves would not fail, and that was possibly the most significant single fact in the continuation of the war. Hitler had, in the past, wavered; he had lost his nerve completely when his fortune was at a crest, but never when it was in a trough. On 28th December in the *Aldehorst*, addressing the commanding generals of divisions scheduled to open an attack in Alsace on New Year's Day, he admitted that Germany was fighting for nothing more than its naked existence. Then he went on:

'I would like to interpose immediately, gentlemen, when I say that, you should not infer that I am thinking of losing the war even in the slightest. I have never in my life learned the meaning of the word capitulation, and I am one of those men who has worked his way up from nothing. For me, therefore, the circumstances in which we find ourselves today are nothing new. The situation for me was once altogether different and much worse. I say this only so you can judge why I pursue my goal with such fanaticism and why nothing can break me down. I could be yet so tortured by worry without its in the slightest changing my

decision to fight until in the end the balance tips to our side.'

Several weeks before in a similar speech on the eve of the Ardennes offensive, Hitler had still spoken as a statesman and strategist bringing his will into play to accomplish ostensibly rational objectives. Now his will alone was all that counted; armies and battles were secondary; what was important and all that was important was that *he* not weaken. He went on to tell the generals that history refuted the argument that one had to look at impending defeat as strictly a matter of the military position – the strength and determination of the leadership were what actually decided whether wars were won or lost. He cited Cannae and the 'miracle of the House of Brandenburg' when Frederick the Great, all but totally defeated in the Seven Years' War, regained by the Peace of Hubertusberg all the territory he had lost after the coalition against him fell apart. Hundreds of thousands were to die while Hitler awaited another such miracle.

On 5th January 1945, Guderian began a tour of the army group headquarters on the Eastern Front. Though loyal to the Führer, he was also a competent soldier and therefore deeply troubled. He stopped first at the Army Group South headquarters in Eszterhaza, Hungary. The Budapest relief operation, barely begun, was tying down more troops and equipment than the Army could spare, but Hitler rated it above everything else on the Eastern Front. Guderian could only urge that it be completed fast. Through the night of the 5th, Guderian's train carried him north across Czechoslovakia to the Army Group A headquarters in Kraków. Army Group A straddled the direct routes of attack into Germany. Its front was on the Vistula; but the Russians held three large bridgeheads, at Magnuszew, Pulawy, and Baranow; and they were the wedges that could splinter all the rest.

Earlier, in November, German Intelligence had predicted that the Russians would first hit Army Group Centre, defending the approaches to Danzig and the frontier of East Prussia. In December the signs indicated a simultaneous drive across the Vistula against Army Group A.

Russian artillery pieces ready for battle

The estimate Guderian saw at the Army Group A headquarters left no doubt that the Russians were ready for the 'big solution' – the thrust due west out of their Vistula bridgeheads toward Berlin and the heart of Germany. The 1st Belorussian Front and 1st Ukrainian Front, the two Soviet army groups opposite Army Group A, had a total of 2,200,000 troops, 6,400 tanks and self-propelled artillery pieces, and 46,000 cannon, heavy mortars, and rocket launchers. Against those, Army Group A could muster about 400,000 troops, 4,100 artillery pieces, and 1,150 tanks. At their points of main effort, the bridgeheads, the 1st Belorussian and 1st Ukrainian Fronts had the Germans outnumbered on the average by 9 : 1 in troops, 9 or 10 : 1 in artillery, and 10 : 1 in tanks and self-propelled artillery. In the Magnuszew bridgehead alone, 1st Belorussian Front had 400,000 troops, 8,700 artillery pieces and mortars and 1,700 tanks, as many troops and more equipment than Army Group A had on its whole front.

On 9th January, after having been given an equally alarming picture at Army Group Centre, Guderian reported to Hitler in the *Adlehorst*. The Führer refused to believe the estimates of Soviet strength and threatened to have whoever had concocted them confined in an asylum. He scarcely bothered to dissemble his suspicion that the army was trying to invent an excuse for running away. He had been a fool, he said, for having given ground in Russia in the first place. He admonished those who 'were beginning to whine' to observe the example of what the Russians had gone through at Leningrad.

That night, after Guderian had gone, Hitler was still thinking of arguments to refute the intelligence figures. The Russians needed 3 : 1 superiority in tanks, he said, just to stay even. They could not have as many guns as Guderian claimed – 'they were not made of artillery' – and even if they did have the guns, 'How many rounds could they fire? Ten or a dozen per piece,' he grumbled.

Hitler was either blind or deliberately dishonest, more likely the latter. In the reports coming to him from a wide variety of sources he could not have entirely overlooked the massive Soviet preparations going on in the last four months of 1944. The railroads in eastern Poland had been converted to Soviet gauge and extended across the river at the Vistula bridgeheads. The traffic had been enormous. The 1st Belorussian Front had received over 68,000 carloads of supplies, only 10% less than had been sent to the four

Soviet army groups employed in the June 1944 offensive against Army Group Centre. Another 64,000 carloads went to 1st Ukrainian Front. At the Magnuszew bridgehead, 1st Belorussian Front stockpiled 2,500,000 artillery and mortar shells and at the Pulawy bridgehead 1,300,000.

By comparison, in the whole Stalingrad operation the most heavily committed Soviet army group had fired less than a million artillery and mortar rounds. Together, 1st Belorussian and 1st Ukrainian Front's gasoline and diesel oil stocks amounted to more than 30,000,000 gallons.

If Guderian's estimate of Soviet intentions erred, it erred on the side of optimism. The *Stavka*, the Soviet Supreme Command, had readied two offensives, related but separated geographically by the course of the Vistula: one would run against Army Group Centre to take East Prussia and clear the north bank of the Vistula; the other, and much the stronger, was to be opened between Warsaw and the Carpathians by 1st Belorussian Front, under Zhukov, and by 1st Ukrainian Front, under Marshal of the Soviet Union Ivan S Konev. Zhukov's first objectives were Warsaw, Kutno, and Lodz. Konev was to break out of the Baranow bridgehead, turn one force north-west to trap the Germans between his and Zhukov's flanks, and send a second south-east to Kraków. Subsequently both fronts would advance abreast westward and north-westward, toward the Oder river.

Strategically, the *Stavka* intended nothing less than to end the war – in about a forty-five day operation, according to its reckoning. The first phase, the drive from the Vistula to the Oder, was considered certain to succeed, and no more than fifteen days were allotted to it. The second phase appeared to require somewhat more daring and time, but not much more of either. The *Stavka* knew the German centre, the Army Group A zone, was dangerously weak and could not be helped from its flanks. Army Group Centre would be driven back and crushed at the same time and nothing could come across the Carpathians in winter. Therefore, in the second phase, for which thirty days were allowed and

which would follow the first without a full stop, the *Stavka* intended to run Zhukov's and Konev's forces straight through to Berlin and the Elbe river.

At the front the troop indoctrination programme had been recast. For a year or more, the central theme had been the liberation of Soviet territory, but soon the Soviet armies would be fighting on German soil. The new theme, in a word, was 'Vengeance!' It was disseminated in meetings, by slogans, on signs posted along the roads, and in articles and leaflets authored by prominent Soviet literary figures. Political officers recounted crimes the Germans had committed against Russian women and children, and statistics of German looting and destruction in the Soviet Union. Soldiers and officers told what happened to their own familes. The object was to give each man the feeling that he had a personal score to settle.

Winter came early in 1944. German Intelligence believed the Russians were ready to move by mid-December and thereafter were waiting for a change in the weather. The clouds, snow, and fog that Hitler welcomed in the Ardennes were not as welcome to the Russians who wanted clear weather for their aircraft and to get the best performance out of their massed artillery and tanks. To the British and Americans, an early start of the Soviet offensive would have been most welcome. In December Stalin told United States Ambassador W Averell Harriman that an offensive would be launched, but he did not offer any more precise information. On the 23rd, Eisenhower sent Air Chief-Marshal Sir Arthur W Tedder as head of a SHAEF party to Moscow to try to learn the Soviet intentions. Owing to bad weather and the roundabout route into the Soviet Union, the trip took nearly three weeks, and Teddar did not arrive until after the offensive had started. On 6th January Churchill asked Stalin directly what he could do to take some of the pressure off the Western Allies. Stalin answered that he was preparing an offensive, but the weather was unfavourable. He promised to commence the attack not later than the second half of January regardless of the weather.

To the Oder

In the early hours of 12th January 1945, the temperature on the front along the the Vistula stood a few degrees above freezing. The roads were icy. Low-hanging clouds and fog would, as they had for some days past, keep aircraft grounded.

On the west face of the Baranow bridgehead, the fifteen German XLVIII Panzer Corps had three divisions, one man for each fifteen yards of frontage. The divisions had a dozen self-propelled assault-guns apiece, and the corps held about 100 in reserve. The front was no more than a chain of strong-points. Some fifteen miles back, the reserve corps, XXIV Panzer Corps, had deployed two Panzer divisions. Two more Panzer divisions were stationed behind the north face of the bridgehead.

Before dawn on the 12th, massed Soviet artillery, estimated at 420 pieces per mile of front, laid a barrage on the northern two-thirds (approximately twenty miles) of the XLVIII Panzer Corps front. After three hours the fire shifted into a strip pattern and the Russian infantry moved out into the openings. The Germans were caught forward of their main battle line; they had expected the Russians to wait for better weather. During the morning the Soviet infantry drove in deep. By noon it had opened gaps wide enough for the armour to come through. The XLVIII Panzer Corps' three divisions were cut up and destroyed. The XXIV Panzer Corps had orders to counterattack, but its two divisions on the west side of the bridgehead were overrun in their assembly areas. During the day, 1st Ukrainian Front committed five line armies, two tank armies, and better than a thousand tanks against the two German corps.

The next day, Konev turned one of his tank armies north-west to meet the thrust Zhukov would be making farther north. The other he sent due west. During the night its lead tanks reached the Nida river. Across the Nida a forty mile wide path to upper Silesia and the Oder lay open.

The German IX Army expected Zhukov's attacks out of the Magnuszew and Pulawy bridgeheads when they came on 14th January but it fared only slightly better than had the two Panzer corps in the south. The Russians were into the German artillery positions before the day was over, and the defending divisions had lost half their strengths. The next morning Zhukov launched a thrust past Warsaw on the north to the old Polish fortress, Modlin.

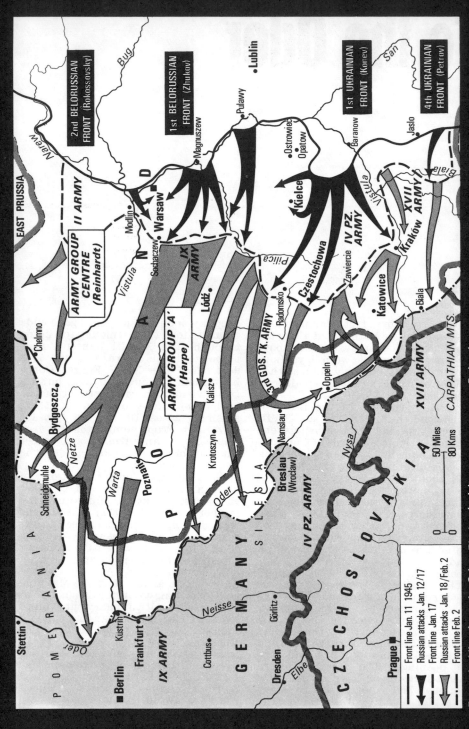

From Zossen, Guderian sent two situation reports to the *Adlehorst* on the second and third days of the battle. The tenor of both was the same: the Eastern Front could not survive without reinforcements from the West; at the very least the Army Group South attempt to relieve Budapest, which was still going on, would have to be stopped and the Panzer divisions there would have to be sent to Army Group A. Hitler transferred two infantry divisions from the West and two Panzer divisions from Army Group South, but he refused either to stop the Budapest relief or to send more divisions from the West. The intelligence estimate of the 15th stated flatly that the Soviet offensive could not be stopped with the forces then on or going to the Eastern Front.

On the night of the 15th Hitler moved his headquarters from the *Adlehorst* to the Reich Chancellory in Berlin. Returning to the *Wolfsschanze* was, of course, out of the question: the Russians were also driving toward East Prussia against Army Group Centre. For the last week or more he had stayed in the *Adlehorst* mainly to observe the progress of the small offensive in Alsace which he was letting run its course even though he did not expect anything of it after he had to concede on 3rd January that the Ardennes offensive failed. Minutes before Hitler left the *Adlehorst*, Guderian called, and as Jodl recorded it, 'Requested urgently that everything be thrown east'.

The next day, when Guderian talked to him in Berlin, Hitler said that he was going to send the SS Panzer Army's two corps, then coming out of the front in the Ardennes, to the Eastern Front. To Guderian's huge astonishment and dismay, however, Hitler stated that he was sending them to Army Group South in Hungary, not to Army Group A. He had decided that the outcome of the war hinged on holding the small Hungarian oilfield south west of Budapest.

Back in Berlin, Hitler once again took the Eastern Front directly in hand. On the 16th he relieved the Commanding General, Army Group A, Colonel General Joseph Harpe, and gave the command to Colonel General Ferdinand Schörner. Schörner was one of the two or three generals about whom Hitler had no reservations. In the Army Schörner, a competent enough general, was known chiefly for an easygoing air that never for long concealed an underlying streak of ruthlessness toward his subordinates. Schörner was the man who would take and execute the Führer's orders if anybody would. Early in the war, while a division commander in northern Finland, he had coined the slogan '*Arktis ist nicht*' (the Artic does not exist).

On his first day back, Hitler discovered that the Army General Staff had put out a directive giving the Army Group A command freedom to evacuate Warsaw and retreat westward inside the great bend of the Vistula. Hitler ordered it cancelled. Fighting from the map – an old habit of his – he demanded 'as a minimum' that Army Group A stop on or regain a line from east of Kraków to west of Radomsko and thence along the Pilica river to the vicinity of Warsaw. Warsaw and Modlin were both to be held.

The next day, oblivious to Hitler's intentions, the Russians finished their breakthrough. Zhukov and Konev had already practically cleared the entire line of the Vistula from east of Kraków to west of Modlin. During the day the remnants of XXIV Panzer Corps, the last island of resistance between their flanks, broke loose north-west of Kielce and began to drift erratically as it fought its way west to the Pilica. Konev's tanks were across the Pilica and up to Czestochowa and Radomsko. Zhukov's troops took Warsaw. The *Stavka* ordered Zhukov and Konev to speed up the march to the Oder and instructed Konev to use his second echelon, mostly infantry that had not yet been in action, and his left flank units to take Kraków and the Upper Silesian industrial area.

The failure to hold Warsaw touched off an explosion in Berlin. Army Group A protested that Hitler's revision of the directive had come too late; the Warsaw garrison had destroyed its supplies and was leaving the city by the time it arrived. Hitler suspected sabotage – not without

Warsaw is lost. Soviet troops fight their way into the battered suburbs

reason by his lights: the original army directive was hardly one which any officer acquainted with Hitler could have expected him to approve. On the 19th he had the three senior officers in the Operations Branch of the Army High Command arrested and subjected Guderian to a long Gestapo interrogation. The next day he signed an order that took away the last shreds of discretion left to the field commanders. Henceforth every army group, army, corps, or divisional commander was to be personally responsible for seeing that every decision for an operational movement, whether attack or withdrawal, was reported in time for a counterorder to be given. The first principle in combat was to be to keep open the communications to the Führer Headquarters, and all attempts to gloss over the facts would be met with 'Draconian punishments'.

Schörner made his presence felt from the moment he took command. One of his first acts was to relieve the Commanding General, IX Army,

General Smilo Freiherr von Lüttwitz, on the charge that on the day Warsaw was lost his conduct of operations had been insufficiently 'clear and rigorous'. General Theodor Busse took command of the army. Others in all ranks would be made aware of Schörner's presence before the battle ended.

Also in the Schörner style, the reports coming out of Army Group A Headquarters after 17th began to exude confidence. The daily report of 19th January stated that the mission of defending Upper Silesia could be 'successfully' accomplished if the two Panzer divisions coming from Army Group South arrived soon. The most dangerous Soviet thrust, one going into a gap between IV Panzer Army and IX Army, would require 'a speedy development of new forces', but it, too, could then be stopped and counterattacks could begin on its flanks. The report did not state where Schörner proposed to get the new forces.

The next day Schörner gave XVII Army the mission of defending Upper Silesia, ordered IV Panzer Army to stop the Russians west of Czestochowa and on the approaches to Breslau, and ordered IX Army to hold between Lodz and the Vistula and counterattack to the south off its right flank. If the assignments to XVII Army and IX Army had at least theoretical substance, the mission given to IV Panzer Army bore no discernable relationship to reality. The army had nothing left but parts of two divisions and one or two bridges. The Russians had destroyed the rest at the Baranow bridgehead except for a fragment of XXIV Panzer Corps that was still reporting by radio from behind the Russian lines and apparently making its way north-westward toward IX Army's sector.

By 19th January the Soviet offensives against Army Group A and Centre were both running at full tilt. The German army groups had lost contact with each other, and in the Army Group A zone the gap between IX Army and IV Panzer Army had widened and another had developed between IV Panzer and XVII Army. East of Breslau, IV Panzer Army was being thrown back to the German border. At Namslau and east of Oppeln, the Russians were already across the border. The XVII Army still had an almost continuous forty mile front on the eastern rim of the Upper Silesian industrial complex, but it lost Kraków on the 19th.

The Soviet armies moved in columns on the roads, scarcely paying attention to the fragmented German positions in between. The tank armies averaged twenty-five miles a day and the infantry eighteen miles. Zhukov's main force struck past Lodz toward Poznan, Konev's toward Breslau, while his infantry turned off the flank toward Upper Silesia. The weather had cleared, and the overwhelming Soviet air superiority added to the Germans troubles. The Luftwaffe had begun shifting fighter and ground support aircraft east on 14th January but its losses, mostly in planes captured on the ground when their landing fields were overrun, outnumbered the new arrivals. Aircraft repair and assembly plants, dispersed in Poland to escape the bombing in Germany, were falling into Soviet Hands.

Behind the front, vehicles of all description jammed the roads leading into Germany. In the mass of humanity fleeing to the west were civilian refugees, Nazi Party administrative personnel, and not a few soldiers; Army Group A did not have enough military police even to begin screening out the latter. The refugee treks, a long-familiar sight on the Eastern

In a fruitless attempt to maintain morale, Himmler lends encouragement to young German soldiers on a visit to the eastern front

29

The Russian army crosses the Vistula on a wooden bridge built by its own engineers

Front, were for the first time composed of Germans. For the first time, too, the treks did not need to be urged onward. They were propelled by sheer terror. The Russian vengeance on German civilians was swift, personal, merciless, and, more often than not, brutal. For three years the Germans had visited bureaucratically administered misery and destruction on half of European Russia. The Russians retaliated with rape, arson, pillage, and wanton murder on their march into Germany.

In Upper Silesia, the cluster of industrial cities northwest of Kraków had, by January 1945, succeeded the bombed-out Ruhr as Germany's primary coal and basic metal producing centre. At the end of the third week in January the factories and mines were still going full blast, as were also the crematoria of the concentration camps that at once provided labour for the factories, and were factories themselves – of death.

To the east, XVII Army's left flank stood like a windbreak, but it was open on the north where IV Panzer Army was being shoved west toward the Oder. On the 21st, Konev turned the 3 Guards Tank Army at Namslau and sent it doubling back to the southeast along the Oder behind XVII Army's flank.

A day later Konev's main force reached the Oder. In three more days his armies closed to the river on a one hundred and forty mile stretch between Cosel and Glogau. At Breslau, IV Panzer Army held a bridgehead. Upstream and downstream from the city the Russians crossed the river in half a dozen places. Schörner ordered counterattacks, but his armies could not execute them.

On the 25th, Zhukov's main force passed Poznan heading due west toward Kuestrin, on the Oder forty miles east of Berlin. The path of the Soviet advance looked like the work of a gigantic snowplough, its point aimed on a line from Warsaw to Poznan to Berlin. All of Army Group A was being caught up by the point and the left blade and thrown across the Oder.

On the right, the Germans had nothing except a skeleton army group Hitler had created some days earlier and given the name 'Army Group Vistula'.

To command Army Group Vistula, Guderian had wanted at least to use the experienced Army Group F staff that had been in the Balkans and was no longer needed there, but Hitler professed to see an authentic if late-blooming military talent in Heinrich Himmler and gave him the command. He had assigned Himmler the missions of holding Pomerania and West Prussia – the strip of territory between the mouths of the Oder and the Vistula – and of preventing break-throughs to Danzig and Poznan and keeping open a corridor to Army Group Centre in East Prussia.

When Himmler arrived on the scene on 23rd January one of his missions was already obsolete. The Russians had reached the Baltic coast of the Vistula Delta, and Army Group Centre was isolated in East Prussia. The prospects for the other missions were not good. The II Army, which had broken away from Army Group Centre, had a front on the lower Vistula, but between the Vistula and the Oder, Himmler reported, there was 'nothing but a big hole'.

Himmler had come east in the *Steiermark*, his elegantly outfitted special train. It was parked first in the station at Deutsch-Krone. In it he had a mobile command post from which he controlled his vast personal empire. He carried with him staffs for his functions as Reichsführer-SS, Minister of the Interior, Chief of the German Police, and commanding General of the Replacement Army, to mention only the most important. Each of the staffs had its own clerks and files. The train was outfitted with radio and teletype, but the sets, fully occupied with administrative traffic, could not also carry that of an army group command. Himmler, moreover, would not have neglected his political interest for the sake of an army group. As an army group commander he had nothing – no communications with his front-line units, no staff, virtually no troops, and no vehicles. For several days on his island of luxury, which contrasted grotesquely with the columns of refugees wandering through the snow and cold outside, he had no more contact with the war than he could get from occasional, mostly out-of-date situation reports. The first of his military staff to arrive was the operations officer, an army colonel, who made the trip from Berlin by car. Several days later the chief-of-staff, an SS general with no staff experience, arrived.

On 25th January for no discernable purpose, unless it was to confuse future students of the war, Hitler renamed three of the army groups on the Eastern Front. Army Group North became Army Group Courland, Army Group Centre because Army Group North, and Army Group A became Army Group Centre.

The next day Hitler relocated the Army Group Vistula, an Army Group Centre (formerly A) boundary. He gave Army Group Vistula command of IX Army, thereby extending its front south to Glogau on the Oder and giving it responsibility for defence of the direct eastern approach to Berlin. Himmler's front, if it could be called that at all, then reached from the Vistula Delta south to Kulm, veered west from there north of the Netze river until it turned south again on the Tirschtiegel switch position, which, laid out along a chain of lakes, was about fifty miles east of Küstrin on the north, and at its southern end, tied in on the Oder above Glogau. The rivers and lakes, though plentiful in the army group zone, afforded no defensive advantages. All were frozen solid enough to carry the heaviest tanks. To defend the Tirschtiegel switch position and the 160-mile line north of the Netze river, Himmler had, on the 27th, two improvised 22 corps headquarters, one provisional corps headquarters, three infantry divisions (one of them a newly formed Latvian 22 division), and assorted odds and ends, including IX Army stragglers, *Volkssturm* (militia), and whatever else could be scraped up locally or behind the Oder. Off the front two divisions were encircled in the fortress of Thorn and another two were trapped in Poznan. Headquarters, IX Army, brought with it one corps headquarters and the staffs of three divisions, but nothing else.

For two days, on the 27th and 28th a blizzard blew across central Europe, piling deep snowdrifts on the roads in the Army Group Vistula and Army Group Centre zones. Then, a day later, the temperature rose rapidly; the snow melted; and the ground, frozen rock-hard only a few days before, began to thaw. On 1st February Himmler wrote to Guderian, 'In the present stage of the war the thawing weather is for us a gift of fate. God has not forgotten the courageous German people.' The Germans, he continued, were fighting on their own territory (to which he added 'unfortunately') where they had good road and rail networks; the Russians were having to bring their supplies forward long distances either by truck over much poorer roads, or by air. The warm weather, he thought, would give the Germans a chance to deploy reinforcements, would slow the Soviet tanks and make them more vulnerable, and might even afford opportunities to 'retake pieces of precious German ground'.

The thaw was in fact something of a gift of fate, although not necessarily as much one as it might have appeared to the Germans. The Russians were, in any event, approaching the end of the first phase of their offensive. The thaw at most put them two or three days off schedule. Konev took Upper Silesia on the 30th. Zhukov's tanks reached the Oder north of Küstrin a day later. By 3rd February they had closed to the Oder from Zehden south to their left boundary. At Küstrin and Frankfurt they were forty miles from Berlin. The Germans still held bridgeheads around both places, but the Russians had bridgeheads on the west bank north of Küstrin and south of Frankfurt.

Helped by the thaw, Schörner was hammering together something like a front on the Oder, and a semi-coherent front was also beginning to take shape in the Army Group Vistula zone. On 4th February in a teletype message to Hitler, Schörner wrote 'My Führer: I can report that the first onslaught of the great Russian offensive against Army Group Centre has been substantially intercepted. The front is still under pressure in many places, but in others we are making local counterattacks.'

Victory in February?

In three weeks the Soviet Army had accomplished its most spectacular victory of the war. Stalin could meet Churchill and Roosevelt at Yalta in February with Poland in his pocket. While his armies stood not much more than a day's march away from the German capital, the British and American armies in the West were still fighting to retake the ground they had lost in the Ardennes offensive.

On 26th January, Zhukov had reported that, if he were allowed four days to bring up fresh troops, supplies and some new equipment, he could be ready by 1st or 2nd February to attack toward Berlin. Konev had said he could be ready two or three days later to carry the offensive across the Oder in his sector. The change in the weather made those predictions a trifle over-optimistic, but only a trifle.

The Soviet offensive had run thus far without a hitch. The armour and other mechnical equipment no doubt needed to be replenished and repaired. The infantry, on the other hand, had engaged in comparatively little heavy fighting. Soviet casualties in January, the Germans calculated, were close to 20% less than the average monthly loss during the 1944 summer offensive.

Because of the relatively light Soviet casualties and the splitting-off in East Prussia of additional German forces, the offensive, German Intelligence concluded, 'Has imposed an enormously greater strain on our strength than it has on that of the enemy'. The January thaw, which a former Soviet war correspondent remembers as, 'Bringing out the snowdrops and purple crocuses in neglected gardens', was the most untoward occurrence thus far. The ice breaking up on the Oder made the river more of an obstacle than it otherwise would have been, and the mud slowed the Soviet tanks and possibly increased the effectiveness of Hitler's bicycle-mounted *Panzer-jager*, but those were petty annoyances.

In response to Zhukov's proposal to strike toward Berlin in the first days of February, Stalin raised only one objection. He told Zhukov that he was worried about a thinly held 90-mile stretch on the north flank where Zhukov's 1st Belorussian Front had drawn away from its neighbour on the right, Marshal of the Soviet Union Konstantin K. Rokossovsky's 2nd Belorussian Front. Since Rokossovsky was not needed any longer against Army Group North in East Prussia, Stalin asked Zhukov to wait until

Rokossovsky had turned and come west. He thought it would take ten days, two weeks at most. The *Stavka* instructed Zhukov to shift his weight west as Rokossovsky closed up and, in the meantime, concentrate on expanding the Oder bridgeheads.

For the German people the first week of February was the darkest of the war. The coming months would bring despair and more destruction but not another shock equal to the sudden appearance of the Russians on the Oder river. Three weeks earlier the front had still been deep in Poland and nowhere on German soil. Now Upper Silesia was lost; in East Prussia a German army was being cut to pieces; Berlin, West Prussia, and Pomerania were being defended by a skeleton army group under a novice commander; and the defence on the Oder was having to be entrusted to armies that had already been defeated on the Vistula and chased across the breadth of Poland. If the Russians maintained their rate of advance, and there seemed to be no reason why they could not, they would be on the Rhine in another three weeks.

In the deepest crises, Hitler had always found relief and refuge in his untrammelled freedom of decision and the illusion of being able to bend events to his will. He did so again in that first week of February. He gave Himmler's Army Group Vistula four missions: establish a solid front on the Oder upstream from Schwedt; stop the Russians at Stargard, eighty miles north-east of Berlin, and hold a staging area there for an attack into the north flank of the Soviet 2nd Guards Tank Army which was heading toward the Oder north-east of Berlin; keep the front anchored on the Vistula in the east; and, lastly, prevent the Russians from pushing north into Pomerania or West Prussia. For Himmler's troops, considering the condition they were in, to accomplish any one of the missions would have been a substantial feat. Hitler ignored that.

In fact, Hitler was indifferent to the Soviet threat on the Oder. He was as convinced as he had been in his first talk with Guderian after returning to Berlin, that the strategically most vital area on the Eastern Front was Hungary, because of the oilfield and because he had also decided in the meantime that the Russians intended to strike for Vienna before Berlin. To him, it mattered not at all that the Hungarian wells had for months not produced enough oil even to supply the Army Group South's requirements or that the main refineries were in Budapest and he had been obliged to cancel the last attempt to relieve the garrison there on 27th January. The VI SS Panzer Army's two corps, I and II SS Panzer Corps, were entraining at the railheads in the Eifel for the trip to Vienna. The commanding general, Army Group South, General Otto Wöhler, had orders to keep secret their presence behind his front.

In the Oder front east of Berlin, in the first week of February, Zhukov set to work improving his positions for the drive across the river. By then, German IX Army had at least something to pit against him – two Panzer divisions hastily transferred from the West and four half-trained divisions that had been forming in the Berlin area, the divisions 'Döberitz', 'Kurmark', '30 January', and 'Gross Berlin'. Their names implied an élite status which none of them possessed. On the narrow bridgehead fronts where the fighting centred Zhukov had to rely on his infantry, and the Germans still usually did well against Soviet infantry. Zhukov expanded all of his bridgeheads, but IX Army denied him possession of the key fortress on the most direct route to Berlin: Küstrin.

Since the last week of January, Guderian had been thinking of a two-pronged counter attack to chop off Zhukov's spearheads on the Oder east of Berlin. To form the northern prong appeared relatively simple. As long as the Stetti Stargard railroad stayed in German hands, the northern assault force could deploy and jump off forty miles behind the Soviet Oder front. The southern force, however, would have to start from the bend of the Oder in the Guber Crossen area and fight its way north through the Soviet main force. The only potentially available unit capable of doing that was the VI SS Panzer Army. The idea attracted Hitler, and he let Guderian bring the VI SS Panzer Army commander, SS General Josef 'Sepp' Dietrich and his staff east to work on a plan. But it was Dietrich's five Panzer divisions that Guderian needed, not his and his staff's questionable planning capability. Those Hitler refused to divert from their scheduled move to Hungary, and before long he sent Dietrich after them. To Guderian he insisted that the operation would work as well as, if not better than, a single-pronged attack out of the Stargard area.

Having lost the Southern half of his operation, Guderian became all the more determined to see through the half that was left. He demanded breadth (three attack groups on a thirty mile front), depth, and speed: above all speed. The offensive, he insisted, had to be readied and executed 'like lightning' before the Russians got a firm hold on the Oder. Himmler, at first, when all he saw was the chance for a brilliant victory that also would reflect on him as the responsible army group commander, was enthusiastic.

In what, for the time, was itself a remarkable feat, Guderian squeezed out of the other sectors in the East and the West two corps headquarters and ten divisions, seven of them Panzer divisions. But to bring together a force that size quickly over railroads operating, when they ran at all, at about 40% of normal efficiency because the engines were burning lignite, and to outfit and supply it in the face of catastrophic equipment, ammunition, and petrol shortages, was all but impossible. By 10th February, the eighth day of the assembly, less than half of the trains loaded had arrived.

From the outset other problems also dogged the operation. Guderian ordered the Headquarters, III Panzer Army, out of East Prussia to take command, but it came late, and he had to leave the command to a newly created Headquarters, XI SS Panzer Army. Under a strict injunction not to commit any of the divisions allotted for the offensive prematurely, Himmler was hard put to hold the staging area and finally had to put several of the new divisions into the front anyway. The upshot was that Himmler and Guderian soon diverged widely on their thinking even as to

General Josef 'Sepp' Dietrich

when the operation could start.

Talking to Himmler on 9th February, Guderian, in an offhand manner he sometimes affected, remarked, by way of soliciting the actual decision, that he supposed the attack would be in progress by the 16th. Himmler replied that he was not ready to name a specific date and wanted to await the next several days' developments before making a decision. Unfortunately for Himmler, his patent lack of qualification as an army group commander left his judgement open to question even when it was sound. In Guderian he had an antagonist whose own judgement was less than impeccable. Guderian apparently had suspected all along that Himmler was stalling to conceal his incompetence. The idea was not difficult to come by since Himmler, in moving his headquarters behind the Oder and refusing to show himself anywhere near the front, had revealed a deficiency of combative spirit that contrasted with a martial tone he had developed in speaking and writing.

On 13th February Guderian arranged a showdown and, in Hitler's presence, demanded that the Deputy Chief of the Army General Staff, General Walter Wenck, be given a special mandate to command the offensive for Himmler. At the end, Hitler told Wenck that he was to go to Army Group Vistula with a 'special mandate', but he did not say what Wenck's

35

authority was. The effect was to take the power of decision away from Himmler without specifically giving it to Wenck.

Wenck, on his arrival at Army Group Vistula, after paying his respects to Himmler, went across the Oder to XI SS Panzer Army to inspect its preparations in person – a worthwhile undertaking, since Himmler had thus far not taken the trouble to do it and the XI SS Panzer Army staff, an up-graded corps staff under SS General Felix Steiner, fell short of being the ideal instrument for conducting a major operation. After satisfying himself that the divisions were in fact not fully assembled or equipped, Wenck resorted to the unpromising alternative of having the attack start piecemeal, mostly, it would appear, to satisfy Guderian. On the night of the 14th, Steiner suddenly reported that on the basis of the whole Eastern Front situation as Wenck described it he realised that even a small counter attack was urgently needed. He intended, therefore, to make a thrust toward Arnswalde (seven miles off his front with a small, encircled German garrison) the next morning.

The one-division Arnswalde attack caught the Russians by surprise, and the division's point reached the town in the early afternoon. It would have taken more self-control than Guderian and Himmler shared between them to throw away such a tempting start. Himmler ordered the whole operation, hopefully code-named *Sonnenwende* ('Solstice') to begin the next day.

Unready and inexperienced, XI SS Panzer Army wasted the day on the 16th trying to feel out the enemy. It was not until late on the afternoon of the 16th that Steiner was prepared to decide tentatively where to concentrate his effort. By then, even though he insisted he could get rolling within another two days, the offensive was irretrievably stuck. That night, on the way back from a conference with Hitler, Wenck was severely injured in an automobile accident, but that he could have salvaged *Sonnenwende*, as Guderian later claimed, is doubtful. Rain and mud confined the German tanks to the roads. Himmler ordered the attack to continue through the

night of the 17th, but that did not help. The next day mine fields and strong Soviet anti-tank defences brought *Sonnenwende* to its inglorious conclusion. The XI SS Panzer Army had gained at most two to three miles by the night of the 18th when a 'directive for regroupment' from Himmler stopped it for good. Three days later Hitler ordered Himmler to transfer a corps headquarters and three divisions from XI SS Panzer Army to Army Group Centre. Headquarters, III Panzer Army took command of the remaining divisions, and Steiner and his staff, currently not in favour with Himmler, moved across the Oder to act as a collecting agency for stragglers.

As far as the Germans could tell, *Sonnenwende* had hardly evoked a ripple behind the Soviet front. The whole operation had come so close to being automatically self-defeating that the Germans doubted whether the Russians had noticed it was being attempted at all. The IX Army reported that the Oder front was 'conspicuously' quiet; the Russians gave no indication of alarm; and all the signs indicated that 1st Belorussian Front would begin attacking toward Berlin within a few days.

Unknown to the Germans, however, *Sonnenwende* had achieved an impact on the Soviet side altogether out of proportion to the befuddlement that had surrounded the operation since its inception. A complete failure on the ground, *Sonnenwende* nevertheless hit exactly the most fragile feature of the Soviet plan for the 1945 winter offensive, the requirement for a certain amount of daring in the second phase, the attack across the Oder. At mid-February, unless the Germans were deliberately deceived, which is unlikely because it would have been pointless, 1st Belorussian Front was fully deployed for the attack toward Berlin. *Sonnenwende*, as the Germans observed, did not carry enough weight to disturb the Soviet deployment, but it also was not, as the Germans surmised, ignored. On 17th February the *Stavka* had suddenly scrapped its original plan, turned Zhukov away from Berlin and directed him to clean out the east bank of the Oder.

Threadbare fortress

The Soviet advance from the Vistula to the Oder in January 1945 had astonishingly little visible effect in Berlin. Life in the capital and its environs, which housed the entire central government and the highest Wehrmacht commands with their main communication centres, continued in its wartime routine, which by then included periodic heavy bombings and frequent night raids by British Mosquito bombers. The exodus of governmental offices, siege preparations, and panic that had marked the German advance on Moscow in October 1941 were completely absent. Russian tanks might be closing to the Oder, but what was to be done in Berlin still depended entirely upon the Führer. Even the questions of how the city might be evacuated or defended could not be safely raised without a cue from Hitler, and in January he was still thinking of retaking Budapest, not of defending Berlin.

At the end of January, in fact, very little had been done to prepare defences anywhere west of the Oder. For political and psychological reasons, Hitler had insisted that military operational control not to be imposed on German territory until the very latest possible time. He wanted to spare the public and, most likely, himself as well the grim reality of having the German heartland officially declared a war zone. Therefore, Keitel, the Chief of the Armed Forces High Command, waited until after mid-January before even giving the Army High Command authority to issue directives concerning fortification and defence of Wehrkreis III, the military district which included Berlin and a broad band of territory east to the Oder.

Keitel did not issue the first actual order concerning Berlin until 2nd February. In it he made the Commanding General Wehrkreis III responsible for defending the city. The Wehrkreis was a housekeeping and administrative command with no permanently assigned tactical troops. The Keitel order merely increased the Wehrkreis commander's authority over troops that might be stationed in his area in the future and gave him command for ground combat of the I Flak Division, the Berlin anti-aircraft artillery unit.

For his tactical orders, the Wehrkreis commander was to report directly to Hitler and would henceforth attend the daily situation conferences at the Führer Headquarters.

At the end of the third week in February, Hitler still had not expressed a decision on Berlin. An inquiry from the Armed Forces High Command to the Reich Chancellory regarding 'the intentions of the highest governmental agencies in the event of a battle for Berlin' brought the reply that the only instructions issued so far were to stay in Berlin. That the city might become involved in the fighting 'or even encircled', the reply continued, had not been discussed. Hitler had said that women and children should be allowed to leave, but he did not want any public announcement made.

By then, however, a partial evacuation of the city was fast becoming unavoidable, not because of the approaching Russians but because of the British and American bombing. The United States/British Joint Chiefs-of-Staff, meeting at Malta on 30th January, had decided that in the forthcoming Yalta conference the Russians would probably ask for air strikes against the railroad centres in eastern Germany. Consequently, the air commanders had agreed to make Berlin, Leipzig, and Dresden high priority targets for their heavy bombers. Thereafter they gave a higher priority only to the German synthetic oil plants. As an advance evidence of the Western Allies' willingness to assist the Russians, the United States Eighth Air Force staged a thousand-plane B-17 (Flying Fortress) raid on 3rd February. The planes hit the railroads and stations, and laid down a tight bomb pattern on the government district. The Reich Chancellory, Air Ministry, Foreign Office, Ministry of Propaganda, and Gestapo headquarters were all heavily hit. Berlin thereafter could not house all of the government departments, especially after a stronger raid on the 26th battered the city with 2,879 tons of bombs and damaged or destroyed more government buildings.

Early in March, beginning with a transfer of Wehrkreis III's responsibility to Lieutenant-General Hell-

Tank-trap defences on the outskirts of Berlin

muth Reymann as Commander, Berlin Defence Area, the planning for Berlin assumed a somewhat more tangible aspect. Reymann's title indicated how little had been done until then: the term 'defence area' was defined as applicable only to 'exceptional cases of fortresses not yet completed'.

On 9th March Reymann signed the 'Basic Order for the Preparations to Defend the Capital'. In large parts of the order Hitler's rhetoric stands out unmistakably. The mission was to be defence of the capital 'to the last man and the last shot'. The battle was to be fought 'with fanaticism, imagination; every means of deception, cunning, and deceit; and with improvisations of all kinds . . . on, above, and under the ground'. 'Every block, every house, every story, every hedge, every shell hole' was to be defended 'to the utmost'. That each defender was trained in the fine points of the use of weapons was to be less important than that 'each . . . be filled with a fanatical desire to fight, that he

knows the world is holding its breath as it watches this battle and that the battle for Berlin can decide the war'.

The 'Basic Order' established Berlin as another fortress. The 'fortress' designation was one Hitler had bestowed with increasing frequency in the years after 1942. Stalingrad on the Volga had been the first. From there west the countryside of Russia and eastern Europe was strewn with ruined towns and cities that had once been Hitler's fortresses. To become a member of a fortress garrison was a *Himmelfahrtskommando* (mission to Heaven), a virtual death sentence. The fortress troops had two standard missions: to hold out until they were relieved or given permission to evacuate by Hitler himself – both of which seldom happened – or to take so long a time dying that the enemy's advance was delayed by the effort he had to divert to reducing the fortress.

Berlin, befitting its place in the Reich, was to be the largest of the German fortresses. Hitler plotted the outer defence perimeter on a rough circle twenty miles from the centre of the city. Inside were two more rings, one about ten miles from the city's

Refugees pick their way among the rubble

centre, the other following the S-Bahn, the suburban belt railway. In each of eight pie-slice-shaped sectors a commandant was appointed. A small inner ring around the government quarter was designated Sector Z (*Zitadelle*, or citadel).

The troop dispositions, however, indicate that Hitler really considered Fortress Berlin a marginal affair. Aside from the 1st Flak Division, which would remain in the anti-aircraft defence until ground fighting began, Reymann had only six battalions, two of them *Volkssturm*, one a guard battalion, and the rest miscellaneous SS and police. The sector commandants would not actually command any troops until the code word 'Clausewitz', the enemy approach warning, was given. They would then assume command of the Berlin *Volkssturm* and any troop units that happened at the time to be in their sectors. Subsequently, they would also take command of any troops that happened to come in or be driven in from the

outside, something which, if past experience was any guide, the troops could be depended upon to avoid.

Hitler was, no doubt, fully aware that Berlin and the German heartland could be defended, if at all, only on the Oder line, not on the S-Bahn. But he delayed doing anything about the Oder line even longer than he did the organising of the capital's defences. As long as he imagined he still had strategic choices – at Stargard in February and in Hungary in March – he neglected the Berlin sector. As a consequence, the front on the Oder was only a little less of a sham than the Fortress Berlin.

By early March, Hitler and the rest of the German command were agreed that a Soviet thrust toward Berlin was the gravest potential danger they faced, partly because the Russians had recently been moving much faster than the Western Allies but equally because they could conceive no greater horror than having the Russians march into the centre of Germany. On the other hand, though, Hitler claimed to know that the Russians were not completely settled

on Berlin and central Germany as their next objectives. That was Zhukov's intention, he said, but Stalin wanted a two-pronged offensive into western Czechoslovakia via Moravska Ostrava on the north and Bratislava Brno on the south, to be executed either before or simultaneously with the Berlin offensive. Where that information came from Hitler did not say, and he was quite capable of inventing intelligence when it suited him.

Late as it was, Hitler would have ignored the Oder front longer had he not decided on 15th March in a flash of 'intuition' that Stalin would choose the Berlin operation after all and might order it to begin within a few days. That night he conferred with Himmler, Guderian, and Busse, the Commanding General, IX Army. If there was time before the Russians moved, he wanted Busse to strike north out of the bridgehead at Frankfurt and 'smash' the Soviet concentration south of Küstrin. He told Himmler to get ready for battle on the lower Oder and particularly to strengthen the Küstrin-Frankfurt-Guben sector.

The apparent imminence of the crucial battle in mid-March agitated the German command. Guderian, in an attempt to avoid adding to the probable final defeat a complete internal dislocation of Germany, ordered that henceforth during retreats, roads, bridges, and railroads were to be rendered unusable but not destroyed – allegedly to facilitate their restoration when the lost territory was retaken. Hitler, on 19th March countered with a directive in which he branded as an 'error' the idea that temporary disruption of the communications lines would not be enough. He ordered a full-scale scorched-earth policy and cancelled 'all directives to the contrary'. Four days later, however, when Joseph Goebbels in his capacity as Gauleiter of Berlin proposed to convert the Charlottenburger Chaussee into a landing strip, Hitler, displaying another of his vagaries, forbade him to cut down the trees flanking the boulevard in the Tiergarten.

In his concern for defending the Oder line, too, Hitler was not consistent. When Guderian secured lukewarm backing from the Commander-in-Chief, Navy, Grand-Admiral Karl Dönitz, in an attempt to persuade Hitler to evacuate Courland and bring the troops back to Germany, Hitler refused on the ground that the evacuation would release an equal number of Soviet troops and leave the relative strengths the same anyway. Neither was he impressed, when the commander in Courland reported that the Army Group Courland would probably be destroyed if the Russians staged one more big attack. On 13th March the Russians had completed the fifth major drive made against the army group since it was cut off in the autumn of 1944.

In another direction, an effort to remove Himmler from the Army Group Vistula command, Guderian had more success. At the middle of the month Himmler almost gladly accepted Guderian's offer to propose his retirement. After the Stargard fiasco and his consequent loss of favour with Hitler, Himmler had evaded direct responsibility for the army group and had finally withdrawn to his physician's clinic at Hohenlynchen, claiming to be suffering from angina pectoris. On 20th March Colonel-General Gotthard Heinrici took command of Army Group Vistula, and two days later Hitler agreed to let Guderian bring the former Army Group F staff from the Balkans in to replace Himmler's jerry-built staff.

Guderian's own tenure was nearing its end. He had lost most of the enthusiasm with which he had come to the Chief-of-Staff's post in the previous summer; further, he had been getting on Hitler's nerves in the same manner that his predecessors had – by opposing the Führer's will. Hitler had resolved to give him 'a long leave of absence for his health' and was waiting impatiently for Wenck to recover sufficiently from his accident injuries to assume the duties as Chief-of-Staff. Lately, Hitler had indicated that he would have preferred to dispense with conventional military organizations and leadership altogether. What he needed, he said, were men like those who had created the Freikorps (free-booting detachments) after the First World War, men who could hammer together units on their own. The best such officers he had at the moment, he thought, were the SS men Erich von dem Bach-Zelevski, Otto Skorzeny, and Hans Reinefarth. Von dem Bach and Reinefarth had commanded the brutal suppression of the Warsaw uprising in 1944, and Skorzeny was a daredevil trouble-shooter, whose most famous exploit was the rescue of Mussolini after the Duce had been jailed by the Italian government. Reinefarth, in March 1945, was the commandant of the key fortress, Küstrin. The two army generals Hitler rated highest were not then available for new assignments. Both had recently been courtmartialled and jailed for illegally appropriating captured property.

Before IX Army could organise the spoiling attack Hitler had ordered Busse to make out of the Frankfurt bridgehead, 1st Belorussian Front, on 22nd March irrupted from its bridgeheads flanking Küstrin and encircled the garrison in Küstrin Alt Stadt (the Küstrin Neu Stadt, east of the Oder, had fallen earlier in the month). A counterattack by two Panzer divisions, originally part of the Frankfurt attack force, failed on the 24th. After that, Heinrici and Busse concluded it would be better to forego another attempt to get through to the Alt Stadt and conserve their strength. Hitler, thereupon, read Henrici a lecture on the 'futility of always being a move behind the enemy', and demanded an attack not only to reach Küstrin but to 'smash' the whole Soviet build-up.

When the second attempt failed on the 27th, Hitler the next day, after an angry interview with Guderian and Busse, gave Guderian six weeks' 'sick leave' and made General Hans Krebs Acting Chief of the Army General Staff. Krebs was known throughout the army for his unquenchable optimism and his chameleonlike ability to adapt the views of his superiors.

On the 30th Reinefarth decided against a heroic demise in Küstrin and broke through to the German line with what was left of his garrison. The fortress was no more, and the Russians had a solid bridgehead on the most direct route to Berlin.

Detour

The abortive Stargrad operation brought the Germans a substantial, unexpected, and unearned dividend of time. In the fit of caution that took hold on the Soviet side in mid-February, the *Stavka* completely dismantled its preparations for an advance to Berlin and on into central Germany, and committed its main forces in marginal, wholly unspectacular clearing operations on the flanks in Pomerania and Silesia. For nearly a month and a half, Berlin and the German territory west of the Oder appeared to have dropped out of sight of the *Stavka*.

No doubt, observing that the Western Allies were still on the far side of the Rhine – which they did not cross anywhere until the end of the first week in March – the Soviet Command concluded it had time enough. This could have provided a rationale for cleaning out the flanks in anticipation of a deep thrust into Germany and, meanwhile, letting the British and Americans bleed themselves out. The sequence of events in March indicates strongly, however, that the pause may have been less a result of calculation than of a failure of confidence high in the Soviet command structure.

There was nothing tangible in the German condition to have enforced caution on the Soviet Command. Toward the end of February, the total German strength on the Eastern Front, 2,000,000 men, was slightly above what it had been on 1st January, but that figure included a substantial number of new, hastily formed, untried divisions and it included also the divisions of VI SS Panzer Army which went to Hungary. Of the 660,000 casualties the Germans had incurred in the retreat from the Vistula to the Oder less than half had been replaced, and by late February a full quarter of the German strength in the East (556,000 men) was bottled up in Courland and East Prussia. By mid-February, the Replacement Army no longer had enough small arms to give full issues to the new divisions. The manufacture of powder had by then fallen below the level required to maintain adequate ammunition production. Against a monthly demand of 1,500,000 tank and artillery rounds, January output was 367,000 rounds. Because of the lack of gasoline, the Armed Forces High Command had to issue an order in the third week of February radically reducing the combat employment of aircraft: the planes were henceforth to be used only at decisive points and then only

43

Marshal Ivan Konev, commander of the 2nd Ukrainian Front, flies to the battle area

when nothing else was practicable.

A strategic intelligence report sent to Hitler on 26th February predicted that the Soviet main effort would be 'concentrated exclusively in the decisive direction – toward the west'. It seemed obvious that the Soviet Command would concentrate on perpetuating the military crisis in Germany its January offensive had created. German Intelligence found it impossible to imagine that the *Stavka* would let itself be deflected from the ultimate objective, the heart of Germany, by illusory threats to its flanks, especially after Stargard. Moreover, with better than 6,000,000 troops to the Germans' 2,000,000, it appeared the Russians could easily cope with any diversions the Germans might attempt and could at the same time carry the advance forward in the main direction.

The German tactical intelligence report of 25th February showed that 1st Belorussian and 1st Ukrainian Fronts' spearhead forces, their four tank armies, were deployed for an advance to the west. Zhukov's 1st and 2nd Guards Tank Armies were out of the line, one north and the other south of the level of Berlin. Both had

remained stationary throughout the Stargard battle.

Between 8th and 21st February, Konev had been in a downright hurry to clear the sixty miles between the Oder and the Neisse rivers. The Neisse was the last water obstacle forward of the Elbe, and in between lay Dresden and Berlin. Until the 21st when Konev suddenly stopped, all the signs indicated he intended to keep the offensive rolling up to and across the Neisse. His engineers were working at top speed to complete bridges on the Bober and the Queiss, and the Russian tank commanders had been issued maps of the area between the Elbe and the Neisse. On the 21st or any of the several days thereafter, Konev could have crossed the Neisse without the Germans being able to prevent it. He did not, but as late as the 25th his tank armies were still deployed for the crossing, 4th Tank Army between Guben and Forst and 3rd Guards Tank Army west of Görlitz.

Between the 24th and 26th the Germans picked up the first signs of the change in Soviet intentions. On the 24th Rokossovsky's 2nd and Belorussian Front, which had moved in on Zhukov's right and taken over the front facing north into West Prussia, launched heavy probing attacks. Near his left boundary Rokossovsky found a weak spot on

Strengthening the line: the Russians clear out Pomerania and Silesia

German reinforcements arrive in Upper Silesia

the first day and by the end of the second his troops had covered nearly half the distance to the Baltic coast. On the 26th too, German agents in Konev's sector reported that 4th Tank Army was moving away from Guben-Forst and toward Liegnitz off the northern border of Czechoslovakia. The Germans then surmised that, as a brief prelude to the main offensive, the Russians were going to eliminate the last traces of threats to their flanks. On the north flank that could be done adequately, as the German General Staff saw it, by splitting apart the III Panzer and II Armies and breaking the German land communications to Danzig and Gdynnia. On the south, in Silesia, hardly anything more seemed necessary; but, since the Russians were obviously about to do something, the Germans concluded they would attempt to throw XVII Army back against the Sudetan and possibly take the Czechoslovak industrial complex around Moravska Ostrava as a quick dividend.

A map captured on the 28th confirmed that Rokossovsky was in fact aiming for the Baltic coast east of Köslin to split apart III Panzer and II Armies. Both the German armies were too short of fuel and artillery ammunition to stop him, and on 1st March his 3rd Guards Tank Corps reached the coast, on the way cutting the road and railroad that were the

main lines of communication not only to II Army but.to Danzig and Gdynia, the supply bases for Army Groups North and Courland.

Zhukov, in the meantime, had not moved, which seemed to indicate he was waiting for a signal to resume the drive to the west. But on the day Rokossovsky reached the coast, Zhukov turned north too. Both of his tank armies and a shock army charged through III Panzer Army's centre, 1st Guards Tank Army heading due north toward Kolberg and 2nd Guards Tank Army turning northwest toward the mouth of the Oder. In four days 1st Guards Tank Army had a spearhead on the coast, had enveloped Kolberg, and had joined its right flank with Rokossovsky's left.

The envelopment of Kolberg brought a peculiar small embarrassment to the Germans. In February Goebbel's Propaganda Ministry had released a film entitled *Kolberg*, a colour epic – the most lavish ever made in Gremany, depicting Gneisenau's successful defence of the city against the French in 1807. Goebbel's epic, in the end, however, escaped also becoming a classic propaganda blunder. The old city on the Baltic, which had surrendered only one of the three times the Russians besieged it in the Seven Years' War and had later stood off Napoleon's troops, though lost at least did not surrender in the Second World War. The garrison held out until 18th March. By then 80,000 inhabitants and refugees had been evacuated by

46

sea, and the last few hundred soldiers escaped on board a destroyer.

By 5th March the Russians seemed to have forgotten about Berlin completely. During the day Zhukov gave the 1st Tank Army to Rokossovsky, who turned it east and began pushing toward the Bay of Danzig. A week later 1st Guards Tank Army was on the Baltic coast at Puck, two hundred and forty miles east of Berlin. Zhukov, having smashed III Panzer Army in four days, took another two weeks driving its remnants behind the Oder. Rokossovsky needed until the end of the month to get Danzig and Gdynia.

The deliberate pace of the Russians' operations in their north flank in March was more than matched on the south. Moreover, what they might have intended to accomplish there was a mystery to the Germans at the time and remains one still. Konev's deployment in Upper Silesia gradually, in late February and early March, assumed proportions that appeared to confirm Hitler's assumption that the Russians planned a major operation in Czechoslovakia as a prelude to Berlin. Indeed, the Upper Silesian offensive is difficult to explain in any other terms. The Soviet accounts

insist nothing more was intended than was accomplished, namely, to force Army Group Centre away from the Oder upstream from Oppeln and back to the edge of the Sudeten. Doing so, however, did not change the situation on Konev's flank enough to be worth the effort and certainly came nowhere near making a clean sweep comparable to the one Zhukov and Rokossosvky were embarked on in Pomerania and West Prussia. Such an improvement on Konev's flank could only have been accomplished by a deep thrust into Czechoslovakia to Olomouc, Brno, and in the direction of Prague behind Army Group Centre.

What probably surprised the Germans most was the complete absence of any evidence of urgency in Konev's movements. For nearly three weeks Konev had all of his larger armoured units out of the front, apparently refitting. Finally, on 14 March, 4th Tank Army and 21st Army moved into striking position at Grottkau west of Oppeln. By then, 59th and 60th Armies were also ready in the Oder bridgehead north of Ratibor. East of Moravska Ostrava,

Red Army infantrymen advance in East Prussia

German troops prepare their defence in Pomerania

4th Ukrainian Front, Konev's neighbour on the left, had already run a preliminary attack for three days. The Germans watching had trouble deciding what to make of the whole affair. Zhukov had all but cleaned out the north flank, and could, it seemed, be ready within days to strike across the Oder. An offensive in the south then, it seemed, would waste more time than it was worth.

Nevertheless, on 15th March Konev attacked south of Grottkau and west out of the bridgehead north of Ratibor, and 4th Ukrainian Front resumed its thrust toward Moravska Ostrava. Konev's armies, because of their overwhelming material superiority, had the upper hand from the start. On the afternoon of the 17th, 4th Tank Army sluiced a tank corps through a small gap in Schörner's front east of Neisse, and linking up with the force coming out of the Ratibor bridgehead, encircled LVI Panzer Corps southwest of Oppeln. That the Commanding General, XVII Army, General Friedrich Wilhelm Schultz, was caught in the path of the Soviet Tanks and chivvied across the Silesian landscape until almost nightfall did not enhance the speed of the German reaction. On the 20th Schörner had to give up the line on the Oder above Oppeln. If Konev's mission was a flank adjustment, he had achieved it.

The Germans, however, believed that the main phase was just beginning when Konev, on the 22nd, turned his attack south toward Opava and 4th Ukrainian Front struck west toward Ratibor. In the succeeding days the Russians gradually reinforced both thrusts, and by the 26th Konev had brought the whole 4th Tank Army in from the Neisse area. On the 30th, Schörner had to give up Ratibor to prevent a breakthrough to Moravska Ostrava. He reported that the Russians were obviously determined to force their way past Opava and Moravska Ostrava into the Moravian basin. Then, the next day, as he had on the Neisse river in February, without having attained any of his apparent objectives, Konev stopped the offensive.

Counterstrike

That the Russians ignored Berlin in March 1945 suited Hitler exactly – not because it gave him time to strengthen his defences but because it afforded him an opportunity to execute a project that had long been forming in his mind. He worried about the Hungarian oilfields, and had sent VI SS Panzer Army to hold it. But he had no taste for defensive battles. He wanted a victory, to make the world sit up and take notice. Hungary seemed to offer that too, a chance once more to impose his will on the enemy. Berlin could wait. When he had thrown the Russians back across the Danube, he would be able to hold them on the Oder too.

The winter had been bad in Hungary, but not nearly as bad as it was north of the Carpathians. In Budapest one German corps had stood off several Russian armies from Christmas Day 1944 to 11th February 1945. At the beginning of February Army Group South held an almost stable front on the west face of the Danube/Drava river/Lake Balaton triangle. Its line was twenty miles west of the Danube at the southern tip of Lake Balaton. Army Group E in Yugoslavia held a line on the south bank of the Drava that still reached east almost to the confluence of the Danube and the Drava.

On 17th February, the day the Stargard offensive failed east of Berlin, Army Group South drove the Russians out of a bridgehead on the Hron river, a northern tributary of the Danube. Hitler had let Wöhler use the I SS Panzer Corps against the bridgehead, which could have served the Russians as a platform for a thrust along the north bank of the Danube to Vienna. On Hitler the taste of success worked as it always had – he wanted more. Throughout January he had had an eye on the Danube/Drava river/Lake Balaton triangle. There an opportunity almost on the scale of the Blitzkreig days beckoned, a chance to retake Budapest, cut to pieces several Soviet armies, throw the Russians back across the Danube, protect the oil field at Nagykanizsa, and shore up the whole south flank. The world would notice that. Afterwards, there would be time enough to think about Berlin. Could Wöhler do it for him?

On the afternoon of 21st February Wöhler conferred with General Hermann Balck, who commanded VI Army in the sector between the northern tip of Lake Balaton and the bend of the Danube north of Budapest, and with the VI SS Panzer Army commander, Dietrich. Dietrich and his staff had arrived from Berlin the week before. His presence in Hungary was still so secret that he was only referred to as 'Chief of Engineers, South-east', not by name even in official correspondence.

Wöhler forwarded the results of the conference, four proposals, to Berlin the next day. The first, designated Solution A, which was tactically the most sound but would have consumed too much time, he recommended rejecting. It would have required as a first phase retaking the ground west of the Danube and north of Lake Balaton including Budapest and, in a second phase, a regroupment and drive south to regain the west bank of the Danube south to the mouth of the Drava. Solution B consisted of an abbreviated first phase to establish a screening front facing north between Lake Velencze and the Danube and a second phase the same as that in Solution A. Solution C was divided into two parts. Both entailed a thrust south in the first phase and relegated the retaking of Budapest and the northern area to the second. Where they differed was on the location of the main thrust relative to the Sarviz Canal, which roughly bisects the territory between Lake Balaton and the Danube. Solution C-1, suggested by Balck, would have put the main effort between Lake Balaton and the west side of the Sarviz Canal. C-2, Wöhler's staff's amendment of C-1, laid the main effort east of the canal, between it and the Danube. Both of the C solutions, Wöhler pointed out, suffered from the disadvantage that they did not provide for adequate flank protection on the north. The Soviet main forces were situated west of Budapest. From there they could easily hit the narrow corridor between Lake Balaton and Lake Velencze and pinch off the southward German thrust at its base. Wöhler, therefore, recommended Solution B.

Wöhler went to Berlin on the 25th. German Intelligence was predicting that the Russians would be coming across the Oder any day, but Hitler seemed not to care as he lost himself in the discussion of Wöhler's four proposals. He was the *Feldherr* again, the supreme commander busy with a plan of his own, not waiting on the enemy. He could even be reasonable. He agreed it would be best for Wöhler to establish a strong flank protection on the north first. He expressed concern over VI SS Panzer Army's weakness in infantry. He agreed with Wöhler that Solution B was the best and the C solutions were both extremely risky. In the end, however, he chose Solution C-2. The attack to the south-east of the Sarviz Canal, he said, gave the best prospect of gaining a large amount of ground fast, and that was what he wanted.

The decision was made. Hitler had what he had been looking for since the turn of the year, a chance to attack. The decision bore a striking resemblance to one he had made two years before, to execute the operation called *Zitadelle* in the Kursk bulge in southern Russia. Then too, at the end of a disastrous winter, the enemy pressure had suddenly relaxed and he had found himself holding a strong uncommitted reserve. He had declared then that he intended 'to light a blaze that will be seen around the world', and he had – the blaze he set had destroyed the German south flank and lost him the initiative in Russia for good.

The German commands now played out their parts with somnambulistic unconcern. No one protested the pointlessness of conducting a major offensive merely to gain ground that most likely could not be defended. Within its own ranks, the Armed Forces Operations Staff questioned whether, in view of all the other threats and dangers Germany faced, VI SS Panzer Army could justifiably be tied down in Hungary until mid-April or later. It seemed, however, to regard Hitler's decision on Hungary as unalterable, and the only alternative it thought of offering was an imprecise proposal for a truncated offensive that would have gained nothing but, perhaps, a slight saving in time. The paper never left the Operations Staff.

During the remaining days of February, Wöhler prepared for the offensive, which was given the code-name *Frühlingserwachen* (awakening of spring). Dietrich was to deploy the II SS Panzer Corps, the stronger of his

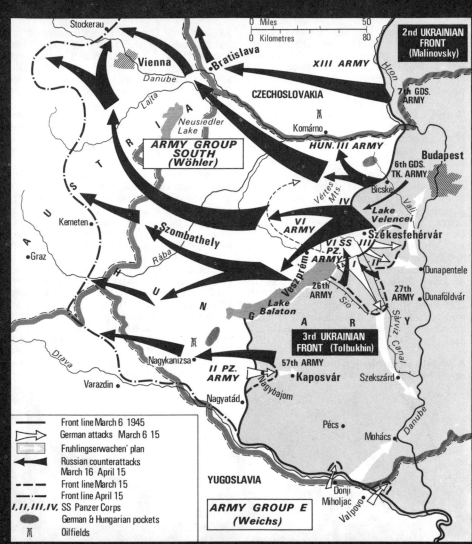

The Germans counterattack at Lake Balaton in the 'Ardennes of the East' – but the Russians push westward to Vienna

corps, east of the Sarviz Canal for a thrust to the south-east. On its left, III Panzer Corps, one of Balck's corps, would push north-west along the south shore of Lake Velencze to provide flank cover. On the right, Dietrich's other corps, I SS Panzer Corps, with help from I Cavalry Corps, would strike south-eastward west of the Sarviz Canal. Between Lake Balaton and the Drava river, II Panzer Army would attack due west.

The Russians saw what was coming and appreciated the opportunity it offered. They shelved a plan to advance on Vienna along the Danube and moved their striking forces, including the powerful 6th Guards Tank Army, to Colonel-General F I Tolbukhin's 3rd Ukrainian Front on the west side of the Danube. There, deployed north of Lake Velencze, they would be in position to meet the German attack if it went north-west toward Budapest and to hem it in on the flank if it went south-east. Between Lake Balaton and the Danube they dug a tight

A Soviet self-propelled gun waits under cover for the moment to attack

system of trenches, well protected by minefields and lavishly supported by anti-tank artillery. To combat the King Tiger tanks, new to the Eastern Front, brought in by the SS Panzer troops, they emplaced heavy artillery. To bring supplies and ammunition across the Danube, they laid a road and a fuel pipeline on the ice and built a cableway at Baja capable of handling six hundred tons a day.

The weather, as the time for *Frühlingserwachen* approached, was the worst imaginable. Heavy snow in late February was followed by a sudden rise in temperature at the turn of the month making the roads heave as they thawed. Even the infantry had trouble moving, and Wöhler began to doubt whether he could hold to his timetable. The tanks could not move under the cover of night. When they tried, they got stuck and could not be pulled out until daylight. On 5th March the weather changed to a blizzard, slowing the tanks still more, and Wöhler considered a day's postponement. He did not definitely decide to go ahead until ten o'clock that night

American soldiers inspect a knocked-out German Tiger tank

when Dietrich reported he was 'substantially ready' and could attack in the morning.

After midnight on the 5th, LXXXXI Corps crossed the Drava and took bridgeheads at Donji Miholjac and Valpovo. At dawn, II Panzer Army attacked toward Kaposvar, but when morning came in the crucial VI SS Panzer Army sector, only I SS Panzer Corps, west of the Sarviz Canal, was ready. The II SS Panzer Corps first postponed its start to the afternoon – and then to the next morning. The weather was warm; the snow melted; off the roads the mud was deep; and the roads themselves were mined and swept by Soviet anti-tank fire. German Intelligence reported to Hitler that the first day's operations showed the Russians had obviously expected the attack.

Already on the second day, Dietrich warned Wöhler not to expect a quick breakthrough by the armour. The roads were so bad, he said, that he would have to rely on the infantry. From Berlin, Guderian, anxious above all to get VI SS Panzer Army out of

Hungary, urged Wöhler to get *Frühlingserwachen* finished fast. 'Right now,' he said, 'speed is of inestimable value.'

On the 7th and 8th I SS Panzer Corps cut through several defence lines west of the Sarviz Canal and gained close to twenty miles. Those and the next two days were the crucial ones for the Russians. Tolbukhin committed his second echelon, 27th Army, and almost all its reserves – three rifle corps, a tank corps, a mechanised corps, and a guards cavalry corps. On the 9th, he asked for the strategic reserve, 9th Guards Army, which had recently been moved to Kecskemet as a precaution, but the *Stavka* had decided by then to let Tolbukhin see the battle through with what he had. The 9th Guards Army would be saved for a counter-attack.

On the 10th in snow and rain, I SS Panzer Corps closed to the Sio Canal, the first water barrier in its path. The next night it took two bridgeheads south of the canal, but by then the German hopes were beginning to fade. Wöhler reported that experience was showing that the Russians had correctly estimated the German intention and 'had taken counter-measures on an equivalent scale'. In another two days, after six days of fighting, II SS Panzer Corps had gained only five miles. Wöhler then concluded that the corps was hopelessly stuck unless enough weight could somehow be added to get it moving.

A day later, on the 13th, Tolbukhin counterattacked on both sides of the Sarviz Canal, and Wöhler predicted that *Frühlingserwachen* would soon run tight everywhere. In the south, II Panzer Army and Corps were gaining some ground, but nothing spectacular. On the south, I SS Panzer Corps, having advanced the farthest, was attracting the heaviest Soviet counterattacks. Anyway, south of the Sio Canal the terrain would be even worse for tanks than it had been so far, and I SS Panzer Corps flank would become dangerously exposed. What might work, Wöhler told Hitler, was to take I SS Panzer Corps back, put it and II SS Panzer Corps together into a drive straight east to the Danube, and then turn them south between the Danube and the Sarviz Canal.

Wöhler must have suspected as he talked to Hitler that *Frühlingserwachen,* if it was not dead already, would be soon. For several days he had been nervously watching Soviet activity north of Lake Velencze. On the 14th, he reported, 'Today there is no longer any doubt that the Russians are preparing an operational counter-attack. The first definitive signs were detected yesterday in the Szekesfehervar/Zamoly area. At least 3,000 vehicles are moving out from Budapest. The intention will be to strike toward Lake Balaton in the rear of the German force.' Wöhler said he intended to go ahead as he had proposed, but, he added in passing, by the time I SS Panzer Corps came away from the Sio Canal it might have to 'lend a hand' to IV SS Panzer Corps which was holding a front south and west of Lake Velencze. On hearing that, Hitler refused to let I SS Panzer Corps be moved at all. It would only end up supporting IV SS Panzer Corps, he protested. Wöhler and Guderian, who again made clear that his only interest was in having whatever was

done done fast, offered all the assurances they could, but Hitler refused to budge until an hour before midnight on the 15th when he gave a grudging approval. By then the decision was academic.

On the afternoon of the 16th, Tolbukhin opened the Soviet counteroffensive on the front north of Lake Velencze. In snow and fog, he made the first attack without armour or air support. The IB SS Panzer Corps held, but the Hungarian III Army, on the front farther north, collapsed; and the next day the Russians began pushing through the Vertes Mountains. Wöhler called off *Frühlingserwachen* 'for the time being' on the 18th; and during the day, the Hungarian line by then having evaporated altogether, he ordered Dietrich to take his army out between the lakes and move it north into the gap where the Hungarians had been. Otherwise, when the Russians came out of the narrow belt of the mountains they would have nothing ahead of them but an open road to Vienna. The last of VI SS Panzer Army passed through the narrows between the lakes just in time on the 20th to escape the 6th Guards Tank Army as it came charging in toward Lake Balaton from the north. Balck's VI Army, most of it still east of the lake, was not so fortunate. For a day and a half it ran the gauntlet between the Russians and the lake.

On the 23rd the *Stavka* ordered Tolbukhin to strike west toward the Austrian border and Vienna. The German south flank was completely unhinged. The VI SS Panzer Army, its leaders from Dietrich down experienced only in executing carefully planned operations, was not able to keep track of its troops, much less improvise a front ahead of a constantly moving enemy. The VI Army was west of Lake Balaton, out of one encirclement but by no means assured of not being caught in another. Balck submitted an ominous report. The troops, he said, were no longer fighting the way they should. Some were saying the war was lost anyway, and they did not want to be the last to die. All were afraid of being encircled, and the loss of confidence was beginning to infect the higher commands.

Eisenhower's choice

The Soviet decision to halt on the Oder river in February 1945 was the most significant strategic event of the last months of the Second World War and one of the most important of the whole war. Had it not been made and had the Russians continued on across the Oder as the *Stavka* originally planned and as Zhukov recommended, the war would almost certainly have ended very much differently and with incalculably different consequences for Germany and Europe. As it was, by stopping when they did, the Russians wrote a surprise ending to the war, one that surprised no one more than themselves.

In January while Zhukov's and Konev's armies were driving across Poland at high speed, Eisenhower's forces worked to reduce the eighty mile deep salient which the German December offensive had driven into the centre of the American line. At the end of the month the Russians were forty miles from Berlin at Küstrin, and the Americans were back to the line they had held on 16th December 1944. Except for a fifty mile stretch east of Aachen, the Western Allies had not anywhere as yet breached the German *Westwall*, the Siegfried Line. In the sector east of Aachen, the Roer river presented a more formidable obstacle

in its way than the half-dismantled fortifications of the *Westwall*. Upstream on the Roer and its smaller tributory, the Urft, several dams formed reservoirs holding millions of gallons of water, enough to flood the Roer whenever the Germans, who still held the dams, chose to open the gates. Hitler would not let go of the *Westwall* and the Roer easily, and behind them lay the Rhine, the most formidable water barrier in Germany.

In the Western Allies' planning, Berlin had always been a will-o'-the-wisp. In January 1945, it was that still. An important military objective and, perhaps, the ideal psychological culminating point for the campaign against Nazi Germany, it had, except for a brief spell in September 1944, always seemed so remote, so likely a Soviet prize as to fall outside the realm of concrete planning. Nevertheless, as long as the Russians were not already there, SHAEF could not devise any plan that did not ultimately also include Berlin except by deliberately excluding it. The last battle might not be fought at Berlin, but it would certainly not be fought before someone had taken the city.

For the British and Americans, Berlin in January 1945 was, therefore, both too remote and too obvious a

55

target to be worth much discussion. The big question was not whether but how they would go toward Berlin. Montgomery had for months been vocally unhappy over Eisenhower's refusal in the late summer and fall of 1944 to concentrate his resources in a single main thrust across north Germany toward Berlin. During the winter, Montgomery's concern found an echo in the British Chiefs-of-Staff who, thereupon, unburdened their doubts in four days of meetings, from 30th January to 2nd February, with their American counterparts in the Combined Chiefs-of-Staff at Malta. The United States Joint Chiefs-of-Staff insisted, as Eisenhower had all along, that there would be a main thrust, and it would be made in the north by Montgomery's 21st Army Group. They insisted as well, as Eisenhower also did, that the Rhineland be cleared first and that there be a strong secondary effort. If there were to be a race to Berlin, Eisenhower would not make it until he had possession of the Ruhr.

In fact, neither Montgomery nor the British Chiefs-of-Staff were specifically concerned with developing a thrust to Berlin, which then seemed more than ever to be securely in the Russians' grasp. Their arguments were as much concerned with form as with objectives. They wanted to be assured that Eisenhower would not again dissipate his resources in a broad front attack as they believed he had in 1944. But, above all, they wanted to reach the ports and naval bases on the north German coast before the Russians.

The battle for the Rhineland began in the north on the approaches to the Ruhr on 8th February. The next day the Germans played their trump, blew the gates out of the largest of the Roer dams, and sent the water surging down the valley. The next day they did the same with the dams farther upstream on the Roer and the Urft. The river was then rising nearly two feet an hour and would stay flooded downstream to its junction with the Meuse for two weeks. During that time the weight of the battle fell on Montgomery's British 2nd and Canadian 1st Armies, operating out of the narrow neck between the Meuse and the Waal east of Nijmegen. The United States 9th and 1st Armies, which were to have joined in on the south, could only sit and wait for the water to subside. In those two weeks, however, without their being aware of it, that strategic initiative in Germany passed to the Western Allies. On the 17th the Russians shelved their plan to strike across the Oder and the Neisse, and a few days later Hitler irrevocably committed his strategic reserve, the VI SS Panzer Army, to the Lake Balaton operation.

As the flood subsided in the third week of the month, so did Hitler's prospects not only of holding the Rhineland but of defending the Rhine as well. By not using the two weeks' grace to take his troops behind the Rhine, he forced them to spend what strength they still had in a much weaker line. On the 23rd US 9th Army and US 1st Army began crossing the Roer. Within a few days the march to the Rhine was on along the whole front as the US 3rd and 7th Armies and French 1st Army began advancing into the Eifel, the Saar and the Palatinate. Hitler ordered his commander in the West, Field-Marshal Gerd von Rundstedt, to fight the battle out where he stood. To withdraw, Hitler maintained, would only shift the catastrophe from one place to another. For two years Hitler had insisted on the rigid defence in Russia, and now he tried it also in the West – with the same results. Rundstedt's divisions were cut to pieces. In the battle for the Rhineland the Germans lost 290,000 men in prisoners alone.

On the night of 2nd March the first American tank column reached the Rhine opposite Düsseldorf just in time to see the bridge at Obersacsel, the prize it was after, plunge into the water. In the next four days a dozen more bridges on the stretch of river downstream from Koblenz were blown before the Americans could get to them. Without a bridge the lower Rhine is a formidable enough barrier to require an amphibious crossing. With a bridge, it is just another river.

On the afternoon of 7th March the lead vehicles of the United States 9th Armored Division, coming out of the Eifel, entered Remagen, twenty five miles upstream on the Rhine from

General Omar N. Bradley, 12th US Army Group commander, crosses the Rhine with his staff over a bridge built by army engineers

Bonn. By then no one expected to find a bridge standing anywhere on the river, but there it was: the Ludendorff railroad bridge, intact and defended by a few engineers and 15- and 16-year-old *Volksstrum*. As the Americans raced onto and across the bridge two charges went off, but the main charge failed to fire, and by dark the Americans had a bridge on the Rhine. Furious, Hitler ordered a counterattack, but in his determination to hang on west of the river he had deliberately neglected the defences on the east bank. The closest division was the XI Panzer Grenadier Division at Bonn, and it had first to scrounge enough fuel to make the trip to Remagen. By the time the XI Panzer Grenadier Division got there on the 9th, the US 1st Army had three divisions across and was busily expanding the bridgehead. On the 11th the Luftwaffe sent twenty planes, an enormous effort considering the state of its fuel supplies, to bomb the bridge. They scored three hits and lost five of their number. By then the bridge itself, which the Germans eventually managed to demolish with artillery fire, was not important any more: the American engineers had laid three temporary spans of their own alongside it.

The incident at the Remagen bridge changed everybody's plans – except, that is to say, those of the Russians. Four days after the Americans crossed the Rhine, Hitler dismissed Rundstedt as commander in the West 'because of his age' and with the by then customary assurances of appreciation and esteem. To replace him he called in Luftwaffe Field-Marshal Albert Kesselring from Italy. On the 15th, he ordered Army Group Vistula to get ready for battle east of Berlin. How much that order resulted from his intuition as he claimed and how much from the perfectly logical deduction that the Western Allies' crossing the Rhine would bring the Russians across the Oder in a hurry is impossible to tell. In either case, he was mistaken. The Russians ignored what was going on in the West. On the 14th Konev began the mysterious operation in Upper Silesia that occupied him for the rest of the month.

For Eisenhower, the bridge at Remagen was a tactical windfall and something of an embarrassment. The plan, painstakingly hammered out during the winter between the British and the Americans, called for Montgomery to make the main thrust north of the Ruhr. The secondary thrust by Bradley's army group was to use only such troops and supplies as could be spared without weakening Montgomery's effort, and Montgomery still had the Rhine to cross. Furthermore, even the secondary thrust was not to be made at Remagen but some sixty or seventy miles farther south in the vicinity of Mainz. If from Eisenhower's point of view as Allied commander the Remagen bridge impinged on the plan and thus threatened to ruffle the waters of Allied harmony, its only deficiency in the minds of his American subordinate commanders was that by itself it did not impinge on the plan forcefully enough. In the third week of the month Bradley told Patton, whose 3rd Army was then on its way through the Palatinate, to 'take the Rhine on the run'. Patton did just that on the night of 22nd, when he crossed the river south of Mainz.

Two days later Montgomery made his crossing. The river was twice as wide in his sector as it was upstream from Mainz where Patton had crossed, but the German resistance was weak since most of their reserves had been drawn off to the Remagen bridgehead; and by the end of the day Montgomery had a six mile deep bridgehead. His two armies and the attached US 9th Army crossed the river almost as if they were on peacetime maneuvers, and before the day's end, the engineers had begun laying a dozen bridges. But, south of the Ruhr, on that day, General Courtney H Hodges already had all of his US 1st Army across the river and occupying a bridgehead extending downstream from Remagen to Bonn and upstream to Koblenz. The next day Hodges began driving east to meet Patton who was coming north across the Main river east of Frankfurt. Kesselring could not stop them. On the 28th they met east of Giessen, and both headed north to envelop the Ruhr on the east.

To Eisenhower, the Ruhr had always been a most important objective. He would not miss the chance to take it, especially not when he could also thereby encircle and destroy the whole of Field-Marshal Walter Model's Army Group B. On the 28th, Eisenhower told Montgomery that 9th Army would stay under 21st Army Group for the time being but would be used to complete the Ruhr encirclement from the north, and when that was finished would revert to Bradley's 12th Army Group. Montgomery would still make his drive across north Germany, but without 9th Army. Henceforth, the main weight of the offensive would be in the centre, with Bradley's three armies.

The plan so carefully nurtured through the winter was, in short, junked. In its place, Eisenhower introduced something the Western Allies had not had before, namely, a coherent scheme for ending the war against Germany. In doing so he unloosed a stormy debate that, far from being resolved in the time still left in the war, was to roll right into the postwar era where it became permanently established as the great moot point of the Second World War. The question, in essence, was whether the emerging political antagonism between the West and the Soviet Union should not have taken precedence over or, at least, have been given equal consideration in Allied planning with the military conclusion of the war against Germany. In concrete terms, the place at issue was Berlin.

Hitler's conduct of the war had raised an exceedingly vexing problem for his opponents both in the East and the West - how to conclude the war with something like reasonable economy and dispatch when Hitler was willing to absorb one defeat after another, always managing to prop up his armies for more. Berlin had always been an important military objective, as the national capital and as an industrial centre ranking next only to the Ruhr and Upper Silesia. For the Western Allies, Berlin lost its

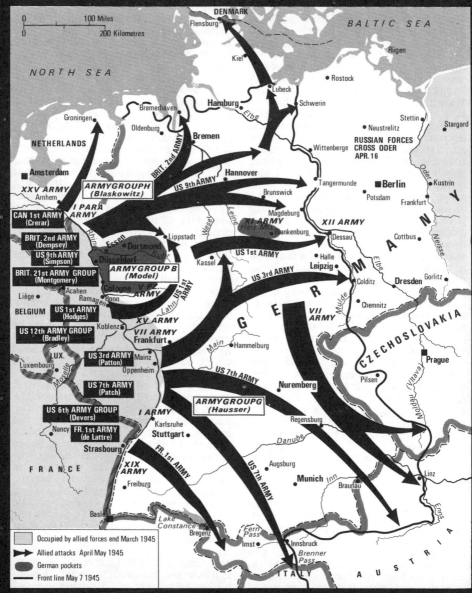

British conquest of western Germany — deliberately halted on the Elbe

military importance at the end of January 1945. The Russians were close enough to take it any time they decided to make the effort, and once the Russians had come so close, it seemed likely that even the loss of the city would not shock the Germans enough to decide the war. By late March, however, Eisenhower had at last found a final objective, the 'national redoubt'. It was, of course, a fiction, an illusion born mostly out of an attempt to analyse rationally Hitler's fundamental irrationality. How else could one explain the Lake Balaton offensive or the determination with which the Germans held on in Italy and Czechoslovakia while the Reich itself was being cut to pieces unless Hitler meant, when everything else had failed, to force his opponents to dig him out of a fastness in the Alps? He might even have some new and hitherto unknown weapons. Much of his talk of secret weapons had been only that, but he had surprised the world with the V-1s and V-2s and more recently with jet and rocket-propelled fighters. He might have others. In another month everyone would wonder how they could have taken the national redoubt seriously; but at the end of March, Germany south of the Main river, northern Italy, Austria, and western Czechoslovakia were all virtually untouched. If Hitler continued to fight the war as he had been, these areas would have to be taken one day. Prudence seemed to dictate that it be done sooner rather than later, and Eisenhower was nothing if not a prudent general.

On 28th March Eisenhower announced his change of plans to the British and United States Chiefs-of-Staff and, in a cable addressed 'Personal to Marshal Stalin', to the Russians. In the cable to Stalin, Eisenhower said he intended to have his forces which then were encircling the Ruhr link up east of the Ruhr at Kassel and from there drive east to meet the Russians, not at Berlin but a hundred or so miles to the south in the Leipzig/Dresden area. As soon as he was able he would launch a secondary thrust south-eastward through Bavaria to meet the Russians on the Danube, probably somewhere between Regensburg and Linz, and so prevent the Germans

from establishing a redoubt in southern Germany.

The first reaction came from London, and it came fast. On the 29th the British Chiefs-of-Staff urged their American counterparts to delay the cable to Stalin until it could be reviewed and, presumably, revised by the Combined Chiefs-of-Staff. When that failed, Churchill communicated the British objections to Eisenhower's plan directly to Roosevelt. What Eisenhower proposed, he protested, would so weaken Montgomery's northern thrust that it would most likely not get beyond the Elbe river, if it got that far. On the subject of Eisenhower's omission of Berlin as an objective he made what was then, and probably is still, the most cogent argument for an attempt by the Western Allies to forestall the Russians there. 'The Russians', he wrote, 'will no doubt overrun all Austria and enter Vienna. If they also take Berlin, will not their impression that they have been the overwhelming contributor to our common victory be unduly imprinted in their minds, and may not this lead them into a mood which will raise grave and formidable difficulties in the future?'

The President upheld Eisenhower, giving essentially the same reason the United States Joint Chiefs-of-Staff had used in their response to the British Chiefs-of-Staff: 'the commander in the field is the best judge of the measures which offer the earliest prospects of destroying the German armies or their power to resist.' Eisenhower, who seems to have been startled by the vehemence of the British reaction, hurried to assure the Prime Minister that, when the Elbe was reached, Montgomery would get American help in crossing the river and continuing his drive at least to Lübeck on the Baltic coast. Eisenhower added that if Berlin were yet to be taken by the Western Allies, the British and Americans would share the honours equally. Nevertheless, the decision was made, and it would not be changed. But the debate would continue even though Churchill for the time being closed it with the quotation: '*Amantium irae amoris integratio est* (Lovers' quarrels are a part of love).'

Stalin's decision

In Moscow on the night of 31st March, the SHAEF liaison team presented Eisenhower's cable outlining his plan to Stalin. In the intervening two days the United States 1st and 9th Armies had all but completed the encirclement of the Ruhr. A third of a million German troops were trapped in the pocket which, measuring some sixty five by ninety miles, was one of the largest encirclements of the whole war and encompassed all of the Ruhr industrial area. Hitler, in the meantime, had recognized that the war was in its final phase by ordering the so-called *Visigoth* and *Ostrogoth* movements, the deployment to the front of all cadres and training commands in Germany.

Replying to the Eisenhower cable – with altogether unusual alacrity – on 1st April, Stalin agreed that the forces of the Western Allies and the Soviet Union should meet, as Eisenhower proposed, in the Leipzig/Dresden and Regensburg/Linz areas. Berlin, he added, had lost its former significance, and the Soviet Command planned only to allot secondary forces in that direction. The Soviet main offensive, he stated, would probably be resumed in the second half of May.

In communicating his plan to Stalin, Eisenhower had desired nothing more than to secure an agreement on the points at which his troops would meet those of the Soviet Union. Although the Russians were his allies, Eisenhower had learned through experience that direct co-ordination with their field commands was likely to be a sheer impossibility, and he was afraid collisions would occur unless the meetings were very carefully regulated at the highest levels. There had already been several small incidents in the air war. His main interest in Stalin's reply, therefore, was that it relieved him of a serious technical concern.

For the British Chiefs-of-Staff the case was entirely different. For them, Stalin's message reopened the whole question of the correctness of Eisenhower's decision. They were not any more convinced by Stalin's statement than they had been by Eisenhower's assumption that Berlin was no longer the most important strategic objective. Very likely, in fact, Stalin's reference to Berlin – Eisenhower had not mentioned Berlin at all in his cable – convinced them of exactly the opposite. On the other hand, they took as a statement of fact the mid-May date Stalin gave for the beginning of his main attack. They apparently also concluded that the

Ferries across the Rhine. Liberator
bombers cover the crossing of Ninth
Army

secondary attack, toward Berlin,
would then come some time later,
which meant the Western Allies
might have six weeks and more to
cover the 125 or so miles they still had
to go to reach Berlin. On 4th April, they
proposed that the Combined Chiefs-
of-Staff 'give General Eisenhower
guidance on the matter'. The United
States Joint Chiefs-of-Staff refused on
the ground that the battle was moving
too fast for the Combined Chiefs-of-
Staff to make decisions affecting it.
Any decisions to be made would have
to be left to Eisenhower.

Free to conduct the offensive as he
saw fit, Eisenhower in the first week
of April began to develop the thrust
toward Leipzig. The British urging of
a reconsideration did not change his
belief that Berlin had lost its military
importance. On the 7th he reported
that he considered it 'militarily
unsound at this stage of the pro-
ceedings to make Berlin a major
objective', adding, however, that he
would be willing to change his plans
and his thinking if the Combined
Chiefs-of-Staff were to decide that the
political importance of Berlin out-
weighed the military considerations.
The next day he rejected a request

from Montgomery to shift ten
American divisions and with them the
main thrust to the north in the
direction of Lübeck and Berlin.
Bradley's drive to Leipzig, he told
Montgomery, had first priority.
He offered Montgomery American
divisions to help in getting to Lübeck
and Kiel but not to Berlin, tempering
his stand on Berlin only slightly with
the statement, 'Naturally, if I get an
opportunity to capture Berlin cheaply,
I will take it'.

But the issue of Berlin was not dead
yet. In fact, it was seemingly becoming more alive by the day. The Ruhr
encirclement had chopped the whole
centre out of the German front in the
West. When Bradley's armies, after
leaving behind a good part of their
strength to clean out the pocket,
turned east they found the German
strength fading more rapidly than
they could move to exploit their
opportunities. The Germans, soldiers
and civilians, alike suddenly were
eager to have the front roll past them
as quickly and painlessly as might be.
Americans had only to show themselves – not in large combat formation, jeep-loads of rear echelon
types were frequently enough – to
bring out the white flags in the towns
and cities. Some places bürger-
meisters and lesser municipal dig-
nitaries went out looking for Ameri-

cans to surrender to.

During the hours of daylight on 11th April a 9th Army armored spearhead advanced a phenomenal fifty seven miles. At nightfall it was on the Elbe river north of Magdeburg. The next day infantry crossed the river and set up a bridgehead on the other side. That same day American troops entered Tangermünde on the Elbe thirty miles north of Magdeburg, and fifty three miles west of Berlin. From Magdeburg the distance to Berlin was only a dozen or so miles greater.

Berlin was back in the picture. As far as British Prime Minister and Chiefs-of-Staff were concerned, it had never been out, and they tried again to impress the American Command with the overriding importance of Berlin. They received some American support when Lieutenant-General William H Simpson, commanding 9th Army, reported that, given adequate reinforcement, he could take Berlin.

End of the fighting for thousands. German prisoners pass Third United States Army transport and tanks on their way to the front

But for Eisenhower the paramount objective was still the national redoubt. He considered it an error to commit any more of his strength in the advance to the east before he had eliminated the potential area of last-ditch resistance in southern Germany. Bradley added another argument against going for the German capital, namely, cost, particularly since, as he put it, the Western Allies would have to give the city up to 'the other fellow' in the long run anyway. He had estimated earlier in the month that the drive from the Elbe to Berlin would cost a hundred thousand casualties. After 9th army was on the Elbe, he still thought the price would be too high to pay for a prestige objective.

It may be that Bradley's was historically the most valid argument against attempting to take Berlin. On crossing the Elbe upstream or downstream from Magdeburg, the Americans would most likely have encountered an altogether different quality of opposition than they had become accustomed to in the march east from the Rhine. At the beginning of April, the Germans had created a new army, XII Army. Originally they

had intended to use it to attack out of the Harz Mountains to relieve Army Group B in the Ruhr pocket. When the Harz were overrun before it could assemble there, XII Army assumed the mission of defending the line of the Elbe and Mulde rivers from north of Magdeburg to Leipzig. On 12th April, Wenck, whom Hitler had wanted as his Chief-of-Staff and who was regarded as one of the best of the German generals still on active duty, took command. The XII Army had seven divisions, including a Panzer division and a motorised division, all newly formed from the tank and officer training schools in central Germany. The divisions were not battle-tested, nor had they had time really to complete their organisation, but they had one quality practically no other divisions in Germany then had, they had first class troops, not the fifteen and sixteen year olds or the over-aged, and the ear and stomach cases that were then the only replacements available in the rest of the army.

On the 14th, Eisenhower told the Combined Chiefs-of-Staff that he would stop on the Elbe. Montgomery's 21st Army Group would go north toward Kiel and Lübeck. The main American forces would turn south and push through Bavaria to meet the Russians coming west along the valley of the Danube. 'It would be most desirable', he wrote, 'to make a thrust to Berlin ... but ... this operation must take a low priority in point of time unless operations to clear out flanks proceed with unexpected rapidity.' With that, the argument over, Berlin finally passed into history.

In all of the debate on Berlin after the end of March – and, strangely, in much of the postwar discussion – both sides assumed that Stalin's reply to the Eisenhower cable of 28th March was a true statement of Soviet plans and therefore the Western Allies could count on having a clear shot at Berlin almost anytime they chose up to and possibly after the middle of May. They were wrong. Stalin had lied. He had obviously regarded the cable as a deception and had replied in kind.

Even as Stalin wrote, the Soviet armies from north of Opava to the mouth of the Vistula were beginning, in almost frantic haste, to redeploy for an operation that had Berlin as its paramount objective. In Upper Silesia, where Konev's offensive ended on 31st March with the abruptness already noted, 9th Tank Army, redesignated 'Guards', was pulling its units out of the front and getting ready to move north to the Neisse. The air units that had flown support missions on Konev's left flank were already moving north, as was 5th Guards Tank Army from the area of Breslau. Rokossovsky's 2nd Belorussian Front, which with 1st Guards Tank Army still attached was fully engaged against the German II Army on the Bay of Danzig on 30th March, the next day made an about-turn and headed toward the lower Oder.

The true mood of the Soviet command, disguised in the deliberate tone of Stalin's reply to Eisenhower, was revealed on 3rd April when Stalin, protesting the negotiations then going on in Switzerland for a German surrender in Italy from which the Soviet Union was excluded, wrote to Roosevelt, 'As regards my military colleagues, they, on the basis of information in their possession, are sure that negotiations did take place and that they ended in agreement with the Germans, whereby the German commander on the Western Front, Marshal Kesselring, is to open the front to the Anglo-American troops and let them move east, while the British and Americans have promised, in exchange, to ease the armistice terms for the Germans.' Sounding very much like a man who had just discovered that he had for too long been looking in the wrong direction – and now found the truth too painful to accept – Stalin added almost plaintively, 'I realise that there are certain advantages resulting to the Anglo-American troops ... seeing that the Anglo-American troops are enabled to advance into the heart of Germany almost without resistance; but why conceal this from the Russians; and why were the Russians, their allies, not forewarned?' Until Eisenhower turned away from Berlin, the second 'miracle of the House of Brandenburg' may have been closer than Hitler ever imagined.

On the eve

After Hitler returned to Berlin in January 1945 he was as much isolated from the people of the capital as he had ever been in the *Adlehorst* or in the *Wolfsschanze*. He had not come back to defend the city or even to share its fate, but only because it happened for the time being to be a convenient place from which to exercise command. He did not show himself in public. He had, in fact, avoided any kind of public appearances after the 20th July assassination attempt. Meetings with the military, aside from his personal staffs, were limited to small, stringently controlled groups. On 30th January, the twelfth anniversary of the Nazi seizure of power, he gave his last radio address, in it holding up the Bolshevik threat before both the Germans and the Western Allies. In March on the 11th, the *Heldengedenktag* (Memorial Day), he avoided the ceremony and, leaving the wreath-laying at the monument on the Unter den Linden to Göring, made a show visit to the IX Army headquarters on the Oder front. Cameramen were taken along to film for the newsreels what was, after all, a rather rare event. Hitler had not gone near the front, not even as near as an army headquarters, on more than a half dozen occasions during the whole war. On the 20th he was filmed for the last time, reviewing twenty Hitler Jugend, boys in their early teens who had been decorated for alleged acts of heroism in the fighting along the Oder. He would make his last appearance on the German screen tweaking the ears of schoolboys in uniform.

After Hitler returned to Berlin and into the latter half of February the twice-daily situation conferences, Hitler's favourite device for conducting the war, were run on a grander scale than ever before. The Führer's office in the Reich Chancellory, not yet damaged by the bombing, afforded much more room than the bunkers at the field headquarters had, and whereas in the past he had dealt with the high commands much of the time through liaison officers, Hitler now could require the commanders, Göring, Keitel, Dönitz, Guderian, Jodl, and any of their subordinates he might want to consult, to attend in person. With the front as close as it was, he could also for the first time, when he wished, deal face to face with the field commands, at least with Army Group Vistula and its army commands. By the end of February that had changed. The Reich Chancellory was hit badly in the big American air raids in February, and thereafter it crumbled under the almost daily attacks on Berlin by British or American planes. Although parts of the massive structure, designed for a 1,000-year Reich, apparently remained usable well into April, Hitler, after the beginning of March, lived and worked in the *Fuhrerbunker*.

The *Fuhrerbunker* was buried in the Reich Chancellory garden. It was adjacent to the old Reich Chancellory and some distance behind the new Reich Chancellory to which it was connected by a long tunnel. The *Fuhrerbunker* was actually part of a subterranian complex. The basement of the new Reich Chancellory was the largest element. Work had been going on in it up to February 1945, and it was damp, the concrete not having yet dried completely; but it could house six or seven hundred people of Hitler's guard and his office staff. From it the tunnel led to the *Vorbunker*. the service bunker located directly under the old Reich Chancellory containing a kitchen, storage rooms, and servants' quarters. In it also Hitler's physician, Professor Theodor Morell, occupied several rooms. From the *Vorbunker* a short flight of stairs led down to the *Fuhrerbunker*. The *Fuhrerbunker* had two other exits, one through a blockhouse in the garden, the other through a concrete observation tower that in the spring of 1945 was still unfinished. The bunker had eighteen rooms. Except for the machinery room and two larger rooms which also served as the central corridor, they were all roughly the same size, about eight by ten feet. The partitions had to be closely spaced to bear the weight of twelve feet of concrete and six feet of earth overhead. The rooms in the central corridor were about twice the size of the others, approximately eight by twenty feet. The one which opened onto the passageway to the *Vorbunker* served as a waiting room. The other became the site of the situation conferences. From it doors led into Hitler's working and sleeping quarters which occupied most of one side of the bunker. The rooms on the other side provided sleeping quarters for Hitler's valet and for military aides, space for a telephone switchboard, and small offices for Goebbels and the Chief of the Party Chancery, Martin Bormann.

In March, Hitler's associates tried to persuade him to move out of the *Fuhrerbunker* to Zossen or to the big Luftwaffe bunker at Berlin-Wannsee. Both the Army High Command and the Armed Forces High Command staffs were at Zossen, in *Maybachlagers* I and II; and they had there the best communications facilities in Germany. As it was, the generals were spending most of their time at the situation conferences or travelling back and forth to Berlin. Hitler pretended to have doubts about the quality of 'Army concrete'. Most likely he was fully aware that the *Fuhrerbunker* was the only place his picked SS and Gestapo guards could protect him. At Zossen or in the Luftwaffe bunker they could easily have been outnumbered. The question of moving to Zossen was not raised again after 15th March when 675 American Flying Fortresses bombed the supposedly secret installation. The 'Army concrete' held up astonishingly well, however. About all the bombs accomplished was to destroy the wooden shells that had been built around the concrete structures as camouflage.

Isolated though he was, Hitler remained as closely and determinedly in touch with the war as he ever had. On 30th March he warned Army Group Vistula that the advance of the Western Allies east of the Rhine could induce the Russians to attack across the Oder without waiting to redeploy their forces from East and West Prussia. He ordered Heinrici to construct a main battle line two to four miles behind the front and emplace the artillery so that it could lay down barrages between the two lines. But he apparently still was not convinced that the Soviet objective would be Berlin. Toward the end of March he had transferred the X SS Panzer Division from Army Group Vistula to Army Group Centre and stationed it south-east of Görlitz, where he thought 3rd Guards Tank Army was about to attempt a thrust south toward Prague. On 2nd and 3rd April he transferred the *Fuhrer* Grenadier Division and the XXV Panzer Division to Army Group South for the defence of Vienna. The transfer cost Heinrici half of his armoured and mobile forces.

Although he was in Berlin himself, Hitler viewed the position of the city with nonchalant detachment. For him it was only one of numerous chessmen on the board of the war. His concept of himself as *Feldherr* required that he conduct operations on a grand scale. Furthermore, he had by no means decided to make his last stand in Berlin.

While the citizenry of the towns and cities in western Germany greeted the British and American troops with displays of bed linen – in shades at least approximating to white – Hitler played the strategist in the *Fuhrerbunker*. In orders to Army Groups North and Courland, he reemphasized their missions of tying down enemy forces away from the main front and denying the Russians access to the Baltic ports. On 3rd March, too late to save either the garrison or the civilians, he authorised a breakout from the fortress at Glogau on the Oder. The city had been surrounded and under attack since January. Breslau, also surrounded, he ordered to hold out as 'an example for the whole German people' and 'surety for a change in the East'.

As the war entered – for him – its last month, Hitler's attention still centred on the south flank in Hungary. *Why* may never be known. He had done nothing about creating the national redoubt that so much worried Eisenhower. He had never felt at home in north Germany, in Berlin, and it may be that he was fighting to preserve the cradle of the Nazi movement in Austria and south Germany. As likely as not, he simply could not resist the compulsion to occupy himself in the one corner of the war that still offered some scope for 'operations' in the style he liked.

On 27th March, Soviet 6th Guards Tank, 4th Guards, and 9th Guards Armies crossed the Raab river, the last water barrier east of the Austrian border. Hitler was sending three divisions of reinforcements, but he had earmarked two of them for II Panzer Army which was still guarding the oilfield south of Lake Balaton, and the other for VIII Army then standing north of the Danube at Komarno. The VI Army and VI SS Panzer Army, being driven back against the Austrian border, were to get nothing. After hearing that Hitler insisted on holding Komarno for the oil refineries located there. Wöhler's chief of staff told the Army operations chief to have him look at an aerial photograph. There was nothing there any more but bomb craters. The II Panzer Army, so far spared in the Soviet offensive, reported that it expected an attack soon. Its Hungarians were 'deserting in droves', and it asked to go back to the main defence line between the Drava river and Lake Balaton. When Wöhler forwarded the request with his endorsement, Guderian answered that to lay the matter before Hitler was a waste of time, for him the word 'oilfield' was 'spelled in capitals'.

In two more days 6th Guards Tank Army reached the Austrian border west of Koszeg/Szombathely. Hitler let VI Army and VI SS Panzer Army go into the Austrian border defences, but made the armies on the flanks stay put. At nightfall on the 29th VIII Army still had a tenuous hold on Komarno, but II Panzer Army, attacked for the first time during the day, had lost Nagybajom in the centre of its front south of Lake Balaton.

On the 30th, 6th Guards Tank Army crossed the Austrian border and turned north towards the corridor between the mountains west of Weiner Neustadt and Lake Neusiedler. On the tank army's right, 9th Guards Army and 4th Guards Army also began to wheel north towards Vienna. Hitler demanded a counterattack to close the front and trap the tank army. Wöhler replied that neither VI Army nor VI SS Panzer Army had the remotest prospect of even starting a counterattack. He would consider himself lucky if VI SS Panzer Army could form some kind of a front between Wiener Neustadt and the lake before the Russians reached there. He had, he said, sent officers of his staff out to the troops; they had all reported that the men were exhausted and morale was low; to expect the troops to counterattack was futile. The VI Army, moreover, was in almost as much trouble on its right as on its left. The Soviet 27th Army had broken through and was pushing south between the VI Army and the II Panzer Army.

At the end of the month Tolbukhin and Marshal Rodion I Malinovsky closed in on Vienna. Malinovsky's 2nd Ukrainian Front, north of the Danube, pushed German VIII Army back to Bratislava. Tolbukhin sent his right flank armies into the narrows between the Danube at Bratislava and Lake Neusiedler. His armoured force, 6th Guards Tank Army, passed Wiener Neustadt on 2nd April on its way to Vienna. The II Panzer Army had by then retreated to a line west of Nagykanizsa that barely contained the oilfield.

Hitler was sending the XXV Panzer Division and the *Fuhrer* Grenadier Division to defend Vienna. On the 3rd, he ordered Wöhler 'finally' to attack the Russians' flanks and to give up trying to oppose the Soviet armoured spearheads frontally. After Wöhler replied again that the army group was in no condition to counterattack and had to put something in front of the Russians to keep them from 'breaking away into the infinite', Hitler called Colonel-General Lothar Rendulic in from Courland and gave him command of Army Group South.

When Rendulic arrived at the army group headquarters in the Alps south-west of St Poelten at midnight on 7th April – even army group commanders did not travel fast in Germany any more – the Russians were in Vienna to the *Gurtelstrasse* and on the Danube west of the city. Malinovsky had brought the 46th Army across the Danube to the north bank and was using it to push west from the Morava river and envelop Vienna on the north.

In those last days Skorzeny, on a special mission from Hitler, appeared in Vienna, hanged three officers on the Floridsdorf Bridge, and claimed that the situation in the city was 'dismal'; no orders were being given and 'other signs of disintegration' were widespread. Rendulic, who himself possessed a substantial reputation for ruthlessness but at that late date did not want to associate himself with the last-ditch enthusiasts of the SS, protested that Vienna was no different than any other large city with street fighting and a disaffected population and threw Skorzeny out.

The battle went on in Vienna until the afternoon of the 13th but without reaching the heroic proportions Hitler expected. At the front, neither the Germans nor the Russians were in the mood for another Stalingrad or Budapest. After staging a respectable fight in the city, Rendulic took his divisions west and north west into the shelter of the mountains. The Russians let him go. In Berlin, in the excitement over the loss of Vienna, simultaneous loss of the Hungarian oilfield went almost unnoticed.

The wonder was that the war went on at all, but it did, on the Eastern Front with a viciousness tempered only by the troops' growing reluctance to sacrifice themselves in a dying war. The Soviet command had its compulsions, too. Among the strongest of those was the urge to reduce with fire and sword the supposed bastions of Nazism and German militarism. Berlin was one of those; East Prussia, the cradle of German Junkerdom, the historic base for Teutonic forays against the Slavs, was another. By April 1945, the war had rolled over and past East Prussia. Almost all of its population had trekked out across the sand spits fringing the Bay of Danzig, but its capital – Königsberg – still stood, a monument to German arrogance. The 1st Baltic Front and 3rd Belorussian Front had tried to take Königsberg in February, had stumbled over each other, and in their confusion had let the German IV Army drive through from the Samland Peninsula and open a corridor to the beleaguered city.

In early April, ready to try again, Marshal Vasilevsky, commanding 3rd Belorussian Front, deployed four armies around Königsberg. The German fortress commandant, General Otto Lasch, had six divisions and Hitler's standing orders for fortress garrisons: to fight to the last man. No one had authority to give any other order to the fortress except the Führer himself.

The storm broke on the morning of 6th April. The day dawned bright and clear. In forty five minutes, Soviet bombers dropped 550 tons of bombs on the city. Artillery, mortars, and rocket-

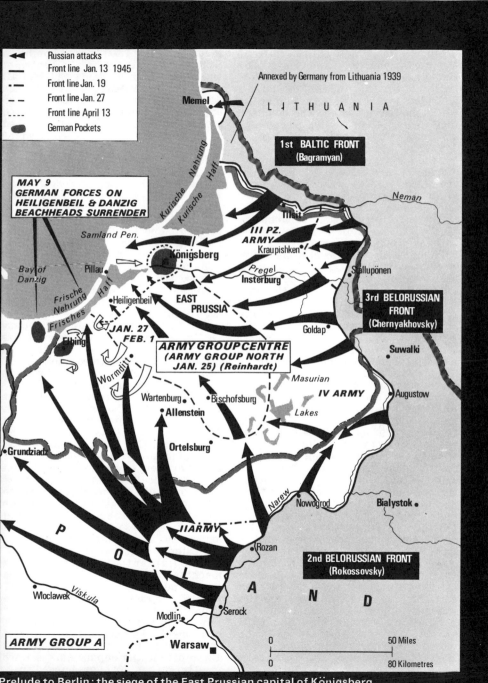

Russian attacks

Front line Jan. 13 1945
Front line Jan. 19
Front line Jan. 27
Front line April 13
German Pockets

Annexed by Germany from Lithuania 1939

Memel

L I T H U A N I A

1st BALTIC FRONT
(Bagramyan)

Kurische Nehrung
Kurische Haff

Neman

**MAY 9
GERMAN FORCES ON
HEILIGENBEIL & DANZIG
BEACHHEADS SURRENDER**

Samland Pen.

III PZ. ARMY

Tilsit

Bay of Danzig

Pillau

Königsberg

Kraupishken

Pregel
Insterburg

Stallupönen

Frische Nehrung
Frisches Haff

Heiligenbeil

EAST PRUSSIA

3rd BELORUSSIAN FRONT
(Chernyakhovsky)

Elbing

JAN. 27
FEB. 1

**ARMY GROUP CENTRE
(ARMY GROUP NORTH
JAN. 25) (Reinhardt)**

Goldap

Suwalki

Wormditt

Masurian

IV ARMY

Augustow

Wartenburg
Bischofsburg

Lakes

Allenstein

Ortelsburg

Narew

Nowogrod

Bialystok

Grundziadz

P

O

L

II ARMY

Rozan

2nd BELORUSSIAN FRONT
(Rokossovsky)

A

N

D

Wloclawek

Viskula

Modlin
Serock

ARMY GROUP A

Warsaw

0   50 Miles

0   80 Kilometres

Prelude to Berlin: the siege of the East Prussian capital of Königsberg

firing 'Stalin Organs' chimed in from the north, the east, and the south. Under rising clouds of dust and smoke, twilight settled on the city. The defenders would not see the sun again while the battle lasted. The bombers returned to their bases, loaded up, and came back again and again, delivering almost another thousand tons of high explosives and incendiaries during the day. Buildings crumbled, streets were buried and, gradually, as impacting bombs, shells, and rockets stirred up the rubble, even the outlines of streets and buildings disappeared in a landscape of shifting bricks and mortar.

The Russians still insist Königsberg was a powerful fortress. To support their contention they can cite no less authorities than Hitler, General Friedrich W. Müller, a reputed specialist in hold-out operations appointed to command IV Army in February 1945, and Erich Koch, Gauleiter of East Prussia, all three of whom at least pretended to believe Königsberg was a viable fortress. Koch was ready to fight to everybody's death in Königsberg – except his own. As Hitler's ex-viceroy in the Ukraine, he also did not relish the thought of being captured by the Russians. When the battle began, he left his deputy in the city and betook himself to Neutief, on the coast just south of Pillau, to spur the resistance from there. Lasch, the commandant, thought only that the Russians were showing the city more respect than it deserved, employing four armies to take two belts of old forts, the most recent dating from 1882.

On the 7th, while the bombardment continued, the Russians bore in from the north and the south to cut the corridor out of Königsberg on the west. At nightfall, Lasch requested permission to break out through a narrow gap the Russians had not closed on the north bank of the Pregel river. Müller rejected the request 'in the most severe form.' Soviet planes dropped another 569 tons of bombs during the night while sound trucks blared out military marches and calls to the Germans to lay down their weapons. The opening to the west had disappeared before morning.

The next day, Soviet planes un-loaded another 1,500 tons of bombs on Königsberg, mostly on the centre of the city, which at day's end was all the Germans still held. That night the deputy Gauleiter persuaded Koch to approve an evacuation of the 100,000 civilians. Müller approved provided only as many troops were used as would not impair the 'continuing defence of the fortress'. Lasch put in the remains of three of his divisions. In the dark the troops had nothing to guide them but the noise from Soviet loudspeakers. Landmarks had disappeared or so changed that even old residents specially selected as guides failed to recognize them. Half an hour after midnight, when the civilians and vehicles began to move, the noise alerted the Russians, who laid down a tremendous artillery barrage on the whole western sector of the city. Two of the generals leading the breakout were killed, as was the deputy Gauleiter, and the third general was wounded. Leaderless, troops and civilians alike streamed back in the centre of the city, leaving now a gap in the front on the west.

Parts of several regiments did not turn back. They had nothing to lose. Many of them died in the two big cemeteries on the eastern edge of the city where the Russians had clear fields of fire. After daylight, a morning fog gave them cover just long enough to find concealment in the swamps at the mouth of the Pregel. From there they watch Königsberg die. In the morning the blanket of smoke and fire was ceaselessly churned by fresh explosions. In the late afternoon the explosions subsided until, finally, they could hear the rattling of isolated machine-guns. After dark, it was quiet, and the light of many fires cast a weird red glow on the black smoke clouds hanging over the city.

In the morning on the 9th, Lasch had consulted his conscience. He could expect no help from the outside. His ammunition and supply dumps were mostly either lost or burned out. Königsberg could contribute absolutely nothing to the war. Could he then assume responsibility for the deaths of thousands more civilians and soldiers? He surrendered; Hitler condemned him in absentia to death by hanging.

Berlin the objective

In the first two weeks of April the Russians executed, apparently with Zhukov co-ordinating, their fastest major redeployment of the war. 1st Belorussian Front had sprawled north during March to the mouth of the Oder. Zhukov drew its right flank upstream to Schwedt, thereby centring it on Berlin, its boundaries lying about thirty miles north and the same distance south of the city. Rokossovsky moved his 2nd Belorussian front into the space on the right. He had not taken Danzig until 30th March, and in the rush of the redeployment to the lower Oder, he had to let the remnants of German II Army escape into the Vistula Delta. Konev shifted 1st Ukrainian Front's main weight out of Upper Silesia north-west to the Neisse river. The three Soviet *fronts* had altogether 2,500,000 men, 6,250 tanks, 7,500 aircraft, 41,600 artillery pieces and mortars, 3,255 multiple rocket projectors, and 95,383 motor vehicles, many – if not most – of the latter manufactured in the United States.

Because of the dark suspicions the recent successes of the Western Allies had aroused, the redeployment and the coming offensive had one blanket objective: to take possession of the projected Soviet occupation zone, at least that part of it east of the Elbe, at top speed. To do that, even disregarding – though the Russians undoubtedly did not – the likelihood that if the Western Allies had made a deal their occupying Berlin was a part of it, the main effort had to be against Berlin. Strategic objective or not, the battle for possession of the Soviet zone could not be won, above all not won quickly, unless and until Berlin was taken.

The plan for the offensive was a three-way compromise. It centred the main thrust on Berlin, but provided for simultaneous maximum breadth and depth of penetration in other directions. To achieve an early start, it accepted the handicap of having 2nd Belorussian Front join in several days late. It also attempted to leave open a chance for a quick turn into Czechoslovakia off the left flank.

Zhukov stationed 1st Belorussian Front's main force, five armies including the 1st and 2nd Guards Tank Armies, for a frontal attack toward Berlin out of the Küstrin bridgehead. The armor was to veer north and south at the eastern outskirts of the city, 2nd Guards Tank Army forming the northern arm of a close-in encirclement and 1st Guards Tank

Berlin burns

Army supporting the encirclement on the south. The 2nd Belorussian Front would cross the Oder north of Schwedt and strike toward Neustrelitz. Its thrust was to force III Panzer Army, defending the lower Oder, back against the Baltic coast and provide flank cover on the north for the drive toward Berlin; but because Rokossovsky needed time to get his armies into position, 2nd Belorussian Front would start four days after the main attack. To cover the flank in the meantime, Zhukov proposed to have two of 1st Belorussian Front's armies sweep north of Berlin along the Finow Canal to Fehrbellin. On the 1st Belorussian

Front's southern flank, a second two-army force would strike toward Brandenburg from the south-east out of the Soviet bridgehead near Frankfurt, cover the main force on the south, complete the southern arm of the Berlin encirclement, and, in conjunction with 1st Ukrainian Front forces, envelop what was left of the IX Army and IV Panzer Army on the Oder and lower Neisse.

The plan for 1st Ukrainian Front provided for two thrusts: one, by 3rd and 4th Guards Tank Armies plus three infantry armies, going across the Neisse between Forst and Muskau and bearing west and north-west via Spremberg; the other, by two armies, directed from the Neisse north of

Görlitz toward Dresden. Konev's primary mission was to be to close to the Elbe on the stretch between Dresden and Wittenberg, where the junction with the Americans was expected. He intended to carry the advance as far north and west as Belzig and from there furnish elements to support the 1st Belorussian Front right flank at and south of Berlin. His instructions apparently were to hold to a minimum the number of his forces that would become tied down in the fighting around Berlin in order to permit an early regroupment south for an advance via Dresden to Prague; but the tank armies on his north flank were an obvious insurance, and a variant of the plan provided for their being turned sharply north toward Berlin.

The Russians did not communicate their plan to Eisenhower although he had sent his to them on 28th March and in more detail in April. After the war the final offensive became so enmeshed in Soviet domestic politics that the extent to which any of the Soviet accounts of it represents what was actually intended or what happened is exceedingly difficult to determine. The account given here is based on General S P Platonov's *Vtoraya*

Mirovaya Voyna (Second World War). Platonov's book had one peculiar virtue: it came out during the brief interlude in the late 1950s when the adulation of Stalin had given away to some factualness (but not objectivity) in Soviet historical writing and when it was not yet necessary to write Zhukov out of the war.

Although Platonov follows the fairly conventional Soviet practice of not mentioning commanders by name, he does make clear that the final offensive in its conception and execution was, as the other big Soviet offensives since Moscow in 1941 had been, the responsibility of a single commander. That commander was Zhukov. In April 1945, the Germans captured Zhukov's order transferring command of 1st Belorussian Front to his long-time chief of staff Colonel-General (later Marshal) Vasili D. Sokolovsky.

The Soviet plan contrasts sharply with Eisenhower's plan in one significant respect. It was a plan for a full-blown tactical operation not, as Eisenhower's was, for essentially the mopping-up of the tag ends of the war. On the other hand, it was not, as the

Refugees stream to safety

Russians have since made it out to be, the strategic master-stroke. Zhukov's and Eisenhower's problems were the same, to end the war against a defeated enemy who refused to acknowledge his defeat. The Russians' contention that the Germans were fighting them and not resisting the Western Allies was spurious. Since February the Germans had been fighting almost completely separate wars in the West and the East. The Russians were simply six weeks behind in theirs.

In fact, Berlin had moved into the postwar era before the Soviet assault started. The British and Americans, the Americans in particular, had observed in their drive into Germany, as one officer put it, that the grass was green and the cows gave milk there too. They had come to extirpate Nazism by as radical methods as might be necessary. What they found were devasted cities, an imminent threat of mass starvation, and a supine and apathetic people. Their mission, they realised by April 1945, would not be to keep the Germans down but to prevent them from going under altogether. In the assignment of the zones the British had secured the industry, the Russians the agriculture, and the Americans the scenery. In both of the western zones the April food ration could be considered adequate only if one assumed that the Germans had hoarded stocks hidden away in cellars and cupboards. The farms were in such a poor state that the summer promised the barest relief and the winter outright starvation. Suddenly Berlin became important, even to the Americans, not as a military objective, but as the seat of the Allied Control Authority, the one agency that might get and keep the country functioning at a level above the catastrophic.

At mid-April, SHAEF had seventy mixed British and American Advanced Ministerial Control Parties, under the the code name 'Operation Gold cup', standing by ready to track down and take into custody any German governmental personnel reported in the SHAEF area. Since winter, another organisation, the SHAEF Special Echelon, had been added to Gold cup. Made up of members of the British and United States Control Council Groups, its mission was to establish contact 'at the earliest date' with the Soviet Command and, together with the Russians and French, begin setting up the Allied Control Authority. In Belgium, Military Government Detachment A1A1 was alerted for the move to Berlin. But nothing had been decided about how the SHAEF organisations would get to Berlin. What was certain was that the Russians would be the ones to take Berlin. Knowing the Russians, the best guess was that SHAEF would have to wait for an invitation from them, which could require lengthy negotiations between the governments.

The Soviet outlook was changing too. After 1941, Ilya Ehrenburg, feature writer for *Red Star*, the Soviet Army newspaper, had become the best known, if hardly the most respected, of Soviet commentators on the war. He had churned out innumerable newspaper columns of hate propaganda against the Germans, interspersed with splenetic articles directed at the Soviet Union's allies. His articles, which could not have been published without official approval, were taken both in Russia and abroad as the Soviet Government's emotional guidance for the Russian soldier. Ehrenburg's vituperation had reached its peak with respect both to the Germans and the Western Allies in the early months of 1945. In the German public mind he had become – and would remain despite his postwar denials – associated with the preaching of vengeance on German civilians in the forms of rape, murder, arson, and pillage. To Ehrenburg's own enormous surprise, as he testifies in his memoirs, his career as a commentator on the war came to a sudden end on the morning of 18th April 1945. In that day's issue of *Pravda*, no lesser personage than G F Alexandrov, the chief ideologist of the Communist Party Central Committee, upbraided him in an article entitled, with customary Soviet ominous understatement, 'Comrade Ehrenburg is Over-simplifying'. Alexandrov condemned him for wanting to treat all Germans as sub-human and for insisting that all Germans were Nazis. Ehrenburg believed the attack had been ordered by Stalin, and, no doubt, he was right.

Hitler prepares

Hitler's world was shrinking. Upper Silesia and the Saar were lost. The Ruhr was encircled. The Russians were driving toward Vienna. On 3rd April, Army Group Courland, practically at the end of its strength, saw through its sixth major defensive battle since it was cut off in the fall of 1944. Hitler, nevertheless, ordered it to stand where it was and draw the maximum enemy forces against itself and, presumably, away from Germany. After Königsberg fell, all the Germans held of East Prussia was the western half of the Samland Peninsula and the isthmus spanning the Frisches Haff to the Vistula Delta. Hitler, who had created Army Groups North Ukraine and South Ukraine after he had all but lost the Ukraine and Army Group Vistula when he no longer held the Vistula, renamed II Army, Army of East Prussia.

The German war industry had all but ceased to exist. Coal shipments had declined drastically through the winter. Already in January the output of tank and anti-tank artillery rounds had been barely a fifth of the month's requirements. In February, the plants had still turned out 2,000 tanks, 25,000 machine-guns, and over 200,000 rifles, but the small arms were not enough to equip the new divisions

the Replacement Army was forming. In March Hitler had stopped all new fabrication except that of ammunition.

The war had come home to Berlin before the Russians struck. On April 10, American heavy bombers staged their largest raid of the war (1,232 planes) on the city, but it was not the largest by much since 1,000-plane raids had become commonplace by then. The new German jet-fighters, when they could get into the air, made the later raids somewhat more costly than the earlier ones, but the bombs fell just as relentlessly. A full third of the total tonnage of bombs dropped on Berlin was dropped between February and May 1945. Of 329,000 civilians killed by the bombing, more than a third were killed in that period. Between 1st February and 21st April, Berlin was heavily bombed 85 times; and was bombed mostly by British Mosquitoes, every night except 31st March, the night before Easter.

In the *Fuhrerbunker*, Hitler followed his accustomed routine. He worked at night, usually holding his 'evening' situation conference at midnight or later, and slept in the morning, until noon or after. The small conference room in the bunker could barely hold all those required to be present, and during the situation conferences, only Hitler and his two stenographers were seated. The rest, great and not so great, stood elbow to elbow, packed in between the concrete walls and the map-table behind which Hitler sat. Everybody coming into the bunker was required to deposit his sidearm with the SS guards before entering and submit to being frisked for hidden weapons. Suspicion hung in the air. Decisions might be announced but seldom were made in the situation conferences. Usually Hitler had formulated his orders before the conferences began. When last minute changes were necessary, he withdrew to his workroom to consult in private with the commanders in chief and chiefs-of-staff.

What most impressed those who knew Hitler then, particularly those who had not seen him for some time, was the apparent extent of his physical decay. His left arm was useless, and his right hand shook constantly. His was the uncertain gait of a very old man. He seemed to have lost his balance, and could not negotiate even the short distances within the bunker without sitting down frequently or holding onto someone for support. For years, all documents submitted to him had been typed in half-inch-high letters on special 'Führer' typewriters; now he could not make out the enlarged type without strong glasses. Some have suspected that the physical disabilities were consciously exaggerated, part of an attempt on Hitler's part to associate himself with Frederick the Great, who underwent a sharp physical decline during the Seven Year's War. In the last moving picture film taken of him, Hitler wore his overcoat collar turned up around his face and his cap down over his eyes, but he appeared able to move well enough. Posed or not, his physical decline was not accompanied by mental deterioration. His speech was indistinct, and much of the time he seemed to be talking to himself, but his mind remained clear and his will was as strong as it ever had been.

In April, Hitler could no longer ignore the coming battle for Berlin, but he also no longer had the manpower, war plants, or transportation to accomplish a true build-up on the Oder Neisse line. To defend the sector directly east of Berlin, IX Army had 14 divisions. Opposite it, 1st Belorussian Front had 11 Soviet armies with a complement of 77 rifle divisions, seven tank and mechanised corps, eight artillery divisions, and an assortment of artillery and rocket-launcher brigades and regiments. The III Panzer Army, on IX Army's left, had 11 divisions; 2nd Belorussian Front moving in against it had eight armies totalling 33 rifle divisions, four tank and mechanised corps, and three artillery divisions, plus a mixture of artillery and rocket launcher brigades and regiments. The 1st Belorussian Front had 3,155 tanks and self-propelled guns; 2nd Belorussian Front had 951; IX Army and III Panzer Army had 512 and 242 respectively. The 1st Belorussian Front had 16,934 artillery pieces to IX Army's 344 pieces of regular artillery and 300-400 anti-aircraft guns. The III Panzer Army had practically no artillery other than 600-700 anti-aircraft guns. The 2nd Belorussian Front had 6,642 artillery pieces. In spite of strict conservation the two German armies could not accumulate motor fuel and ammunition at anywhere near the rate needed for a major operation. On 11th April, the artillery ammunition in the Army Group Vistula zone stood at 0·9 of a basic load. The 1st and 2nd Belorussian Fronts had 3·2 and 1·9 basic loads as initial issues for their vastly greater arrays of guns. The III Panzer Army and IX Army were nothing like the forces they had been in 1941 when they marched out of Poland and across European Russia to the gates of Moscow. The names were the same; the men were gone, dead, crippled, or prisoners of the Soviet Union; and the equipment was lost in the snows of four winters, in the swamps of Belorussia, and on the banks of the Vistula and the Neman.

Hitler did little to compensate for the deficiencies. He ordered the anti-aircraft guns, most of which were taken from the Berlin air defence, emplaced so that they could fire on ground targets. The armies added depth to the front by constructing the *Wot an* position ten to fifteen miles to the rear of the Oder line. Hitler

promised Heinrici 100,000 troops to replace the panzer divisions transferred to Army Group South and Centre. He delivered about 35,000 untrained Navy and Luftwaffe men.

The total German situation was too uncertain to permit any coherent planning in the event the defence on the rivers failed. The one overriding objective left was to prolong the war. Hitler had never been more firmly in command, and as long as he lived there was no way out short of total defeat in the field – or the miracle he predicted.

Anticipating a junction between the Western Allies and the Russians that would split Germany in two, Hitler, on 10th and 14th April, issued orders naming Dönitz commander in chief in the north and Kesselring in the south. The appointments were to take effect after contact between the two areas was broken. Hitler expected to retain the supreme command in one or the other himself. On 11th April, German troops captured a copy of the SHAEF 'Eclipse' order. 'Eclipse' was the code word for the end of German resistance, and the order attempted

Civilians and police help prepare the defences

to provide guidance for the British and United States commanders tailored to the various conditions that might prevail when the end came. Hitler learned from it the hitherto Top Secret arrangement of the zones. The thought of the Western Allies and the Soviet Union confronting each other in central Germany seemed almost to please him.

Hitler transferred command of the Berlin city defence to Army Group Vistula on 15th April. Until then the Berlin command had been directly under him, but he had ignored it. On the night of the 15th, at the army group headquarters, the Berlin commander, Reymann, took part in what for him must have been a dismayingly painful conference. Dr Albert Speer, the Minister of Armament and Munitions and formerly Hitler's chief architect, was there too. He was on a barnstorming tour of the field commands trying to persuade the generals to execute the scorched earth policy Hitler had ordered in March.

77

Reymann had, on orders from Goebbels as Gauleiter of Berlin, placed hundreds of explosive charges throughout the city. Speer told him that the destruction of the bridges and other municipal facilities would have highly doubtful military value but was certain to cause starvation, epidemics, and an economic collapse that might take years to overcome. Heinrici agreed and added that, if the time came when a choice had to be made, the army group did not propose to fight in the city; IX Army would retreat past it on both sides.

At mid-month, aside from the by then obvious 1st Belorussian Front concentration east of Berlin, the Germans had only a hazy and, in one important respect, completely false picture of the Soviet deployment and intentions. Hitler and the Army Group Centre commander, Schörner – who took his cue from the Führer – had become convinced in late March that the Russians would try both the so-called Zhukov (Berlin) and Stalin (Prague) offensive solutions, the ones Hitler had claimed to have knowledge of earlier in the month. In early April, German Intelligence lost track of the 3rd Guards Tank Army and assumed it to be east of Bunzlau where it would have been deployed had it proposed to attack south toward Zittau into the gap between the Erzgebirge and the Sudetan and thence toward Prague. On 10th April, Schörner – awarded his marshal's baton five days before, which gave him the dubious distinction of being the first German general to attain the rank since Freidrich Paulus was promoted at Stalingrad – told Hitler, 'It is to be assumed that the enemy attack will be centered in the area between Görlitz and Löwenberg [that is, south-west of Bunzlau]'. The German intelligence estimate of 13th April hedged a bit on where the attack would come against Army Group Centre but reached essentially the same conclusion: that 1st Ukrainian Front's main offensive concentration was northeast of Görlitz/Löwenberg. Consequently, when the Soviet offensive began Schörner was holding half of his reserves, two Panzer divisions, fifty miles south-east of the Soviet main thrust.

On 11th April, Hitler, advised Heinrici to order his army group into its main battle formation that night or the next. The Americans, he explained, had reached Magdeburg that day; the Russians, if they wanted to take their share of Germany, might be forced to attack before they were ready. Having by then seen the Eclipse order, Hitler apparently assumed – or hoped – that the appearance of the Americans inside the proposed Soviet zone signalled the beginning of a scramble for the Soviet share of Germany.

On the 12th Krebs told the Army Group Vistula operations officer that the Führer was convinced the army group would have a 'colossal' victory; nowhere in Germany was a front so strongly held or so well supplied with ammunition. The operations officer replied that the Führer should also consider the enemy's strength, that the ammunition the army group had could hardly last for the expected long fight, and that its motor fuel was already short.

Two days later, on the 14th, five Soviet divisions and two hundred tanks tried unsuccessfully to storm the Seelow Heights west of Köstrin. When the Russians did not try again the next day, Heinrici thought they might have decided to wait a while longer with their big offensive. He considered ordering the troops out of the main battle line and back into the original front, but decided not to because the previous day's attack had showed that they were 'clinging' to the main battle line and needed every physical support they could be given.

Hitler in an order of the day on the 14th ranted about traitorous German officers in Russian pay and German women who would be reduced by the Russians to barrack whores, and pretended to see the hand of benign power in the death two days before of 'the greatest war criminal of all time' (Roosevelt) and boasted that he had done so much since January to strengthen the front 'that the Bolsheviks this time too will suffer the old fate of Asia and bleed to death before the German capital'. He called for the defence 'not of the empty concept of the Fatherland but of your homes, your women, your children, and thereby our future'.

Battle on the Oder

In wartime, if they learn nothing else, human beings learn to adjust. The Russians were thirty five miles from Berlin, but they had been there since the end of January, and their presence had somehow become one of commonplaces of the city's life, along with nightly raids by the Mosquitoes, less frequent but more terrifying daylight B-17 raids, existence in the air raid shelters, and not knowing from hour to hour what might happen to one's home, one's family, or oneself. Goebbels filled the radio news programmes with atrocity stories, including a much discussed report by a refugee from East Prussia who claimed to have been raped *exactly* twenty four times. The Berliners were content to meet one fate at a time, and for the moment there seemed to be none worse than death. In the air raid shelters they said, 'Better Russians on the belly than the "*Amis*" on the head'.

The German Supreme Command was located closer to the front than would formerly have been considered proper for an army group headquarters; yet every day cavalcades of cars travelled back and forth to the Reich Chancellory from the headquarters scattered in and about the city. In the *Fuhrerbunker*, except for the Führer's frequent meanderings, many of which had nothing to do with the current state of the war at all, the discussions were conducted on an astringent professional plane that, considering the subject matter, now seems almost comically irrational. For instance, on 4th April, Dönitz reported to Hitler that in the past five days' bombing raids the Navy had lost in the docks and harbours twenty-four U-boats; the pocket-battleship *Sheer* had capsized; the heavy cruiser *Hipper* had set afire; and the light cruiser *Emden* had been damaged. Dönitz remarked that the Navy's recent losses had been almost exclusively in the harbours. Hitler reminded him, possibly with some irony, that the Navy's earlier losses had also been mostly the result of enemy air action. With that the discussion ended.

But the war would go on; the hour of decision was approaching, everyone knew that. In the second week of April a new face appeared in the *Fuhrerbunker*, one that some even of those who had long access to Hitler's official circle did not recognise. Eva Braun, whose relationship to Hitler had been so well concealed that its real nature is still mostly a matter of conjecture, had come from the comparative safety

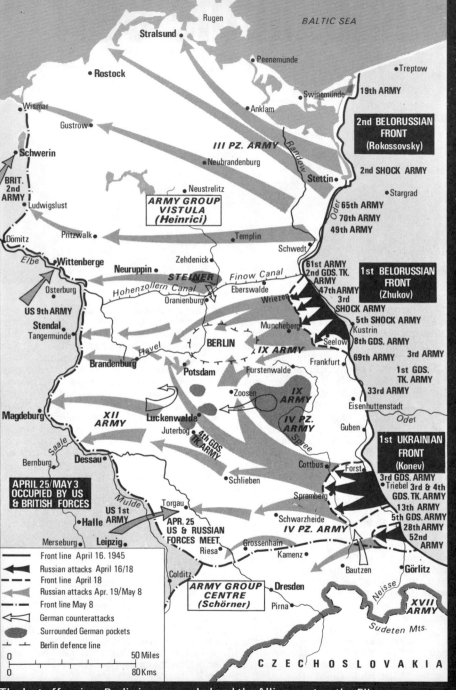

The last offensive: Berlin is surrounded and the Allies meet on the Elbe

**Tanks of the 1st Belorussian Front
parade before a night attack**

of Munich determined to share whatever befell him. Moderately pretty but no beauty, agreeable but by no means intelligent, she did not fit the picture of a great man's mistress. And it apparently was neither deep love nor a sense of the dramatic that brought her to Berlin. Although she had attempted suicide once and threatened it several times, although she had become wealthy from her share in the profits of the sale of Hitler photographs, she remained what she had been, a German petty-*bourgeois* with an intense personal longing for respectability and a schoolgirl loyalty to Hitler, not as a lover but as the Führer. It was apparently a combination of the two that brought her to Berlin. To Heinrich Hoffman, Hitler's personal photographer and her business partner, she said, 'What would people say if I left him now in time of trouble?' Nevertheless, hers was a loyalty that would be matched among Hitler's closest associates only by one other – Goebbels.

The time of waiting ended in the early hours of 16th April. The 1st Belorussian Front attacked before dawn that morning, and 1st Ukrainian Front joined in at daylight. The 1st Belorussian Front, the stronger, also had by far the tougher assignment. Its main force, deployed in a twenty mile sector between Wriezen and Seelow had to cross the marshy bottomland of the Oder and the Alte Oder and take the Seelow Heights, the line of bluffs a mile or two west of the river. The attack began in darkness – to achieve surprise – and batteries of powerful searchlights had been positioned to illuminate the German line and blind the defenders. The infantry moved out behind a shattering artillery preparation, but the lights did not have the expected effect. Flashing into the early morning haze and the smoke of the explosions they made a spectacular but useless display. In the mud, smoke, and darkness the waves of Russian infantry piled up on each other. By daylight, the confusion was complete. The Russians were lucky that the Germans, nervous and preoccupied, failed to appreciate what was happening and so left them to work out their problem by themselves.

During the day, apparently on orders from Stalin, Sokolovsky comitted the 1st and 2nd Guards Tank Armies, which could not help tactically since the German line was not broken anywhere, but which added mightily to the tangle as the armour

Soviet infantrymen advance through wooded country

tried to push forward. At nightfall the divisions that had charged in the morning behind unfurled banners were all still in front of the German main battle line, and to make the day complete, neither of 1st Belorussian Front's flank forces had any success either. At his famous victory press conference in June 1945 Zhukov said, with no indication of intentional humour, 'It was an interesting and instructive battle, especially as regards tempos and the technique of night-fighting on such a scale'.

The performance was, in fact, little short of comic opera played on a twenty mile-wide stage. But though the Russians could afford their mistakes, the Germans could not afford theirs. Against IV Panzer Army on Schörner's left flank, Konev's infantry crossed the Neisse between Muskau and Forst and north of Görlitz, penetrating as deep as six miles on the first day while Schorner's two reserve Panzer divisions lingered fifty miles to the south.

After the 3rd and 5th Shock Armies and 8th Guards Army again failed to get moving on the morning of the second day, Sokolovsky threw in a reserve army – 47th Army – and both tank armies and zeroed in on two small areas, southeast of Wriezen and at Seelow. Two reserve Panzer divisions, although slowed by air attacks, arrived in time to hold them to minor gains. At the end of the second day, the march

on Berlin was still mired in the Oder swamps.

On the 18th, Sokolovsky drew his armour together more tightly and broke in ten to twelve miles west of Wriezen and south-west of Seelow, but IX Army still held its front together through the day. Heinrici reported, however, that the battle was approaching its climax and soon would be decided.

The Russians were straining to the utmost, putting service troops into the front and threatening the death penalty for failure to advance on orders. Such threats had not often had to be made in the years since 1942, and the Germans were not fighting as well as they had on many other occasions. Zhukov – according

to the Soviet official history – had already changed the plan on the 17th and had ordered Konev's 3rd and 4th Guards Tank Armies to strike for Berlin as soon as they were in the clear. He had also ordered 2nd Belorussian Front, not yet in action, to direct its advance southwest instead of northwest so as to complete the Berlin encirclement on the north in case 1st Belorussian Front failed to get through.

At the end of the third, Konev's northern force was on the Spree River north and south of Spremberg and across the river south of the city. His southern force was approaching Bautzen. Schörner also reported that the battle was reaching its climax in his zone. He thought the Russian's heavy losses might exhaust their ability to keep up the attack, and he intended to put his last troop and ammunition reserves into counterattacks the next day.

In the *Fuhrerbunker* the 18th was a day of optimism. At the situation conference held in the small hours of the morning, Hitler expressed the belief that the offensive against IV Panzer Army on Schörner's front had 'substantially' run itself tight. Dönitz's adjutant recorded that 'the voices of hope were loud'. As far as he could determine, however, much of the optimism seemed to be founded on a principle Keitel had recently invented, namely, that offensives invariably stalled if they had not made the breakthrough by the end of the third day. Hitler told Colonel-General Karl Hilpert, Commanding General Army Group Courland, who came to Berlin that day, that his army group would have to hold out 'until the turn that has occurred in every war has taken place'.

The next day the south group of 1st Belorussian Front's main force got as far as Muncheberg twenty miles due east of Berlin. The northern group, 2nd Guards Tank Army in the van, broke through west of Wriezen. It could have gone faster and farther, but the flank covering force was not yet out of the bridgehead. Hitler, determined to fight out the battle for Berlin on the IX Army front, gave Heinrici permission to take all the combat-worthy troops he could find out of the Berlin city defences.

Meanwhile, Konev was putting his armour across the Spree north and south of Spremberg in accordance with the changed plan. South of Spremberg IV Panzer Army still had a vestige of a front; north of the city almost the whole 3rd Guards Tank Army was across the Spree. Schörner reported that he had 'hopes' of stopping Konev's southern thrust toward Bautzen. He intended to try again to close the front on the north; but, he added, 'The laboriously organized defence in depth has only accomplished in a few places what one was forced to promise oneself from it'.

On the 20th Hitler's birthday, the battle for Berlin was lost. The 3rd and 4th Guards Tank Armies pulled away from the Army Group Centre flank and by day's end had strong armored spearheads thrusting north past Juterbog, the Army's largest ammunition depot, and closing up to the German screening line ten miles south of Zossen. The 2nd Belorussian Front joined the offensive during the day, attacking across the Oder on almost the whole front from Stettin to Schwedt under the cover of smoke and creating several bridgeheads. North of Berlin, 2nd Guards Tank Army reached Bernau, on the Berlin-Stettin *Autobahn* ten miles north of the capital. The southern group of 1st Belorussian Front's main force was still having trouble pushing toward Berlin, but it got a spearhead through to the southwest past Muncheberg to Furstenwalde, behind IX Army.

Busse, the Commanding General, IX Army, reported in the morning that the only way he could get a solid front east of Berlin was by taking his line back from the Oder at and south of Frankfurt. No reply came from Hitler until late in the afternoon when Krebs called Heinrici to say that Hitler doubted whether the troops, and particularly whether the heavy anti-aircraft guns, could be withdrawn from the Oder, and wanted to talk to him before making a decision. The army group chief-of-staff replied that Heinrici was away at the front but said that he could not be responsible for mastering the situation if the order to take IX Army back were not given soon.

By then the Russians were approaching Furstenwalde. During the early half of the night, by telephoned commands relayed through Krebs and the Army General Staff Operations Branch, Hitler tried to juggle divisions to stop the Russians at Bernau and Furstenwalde. Half an hour after midnight Heinrici returned to his headquarters, called Krebs, and told him that Hitler now had ordered the army group to hold everywhere, and at the same time to take troops out to protect the threatened flanks. He was convinced that the missions could not be fulfilled and would 'never succeed'. He proposed to go to the Führer and tell him so, and ask to be relieved and allowed to 'take up a rifle and face the enemy'.

The encirclement

The observance of the Führer's birthday was subdued, but, even so, it was conducted with more ceremony than was appropriate to the German condition. On the night of the 19th, as he had for twelve years past, Goebbels gave the birthday radio address and ended it as he had the others with a loud 'Our Hitler!' The speech itself was mostly a mish-mash of exculpatory allusions to 'the work of the Devil', 'Satanic powers', and 'the perverse coalition of plutocracy and Bolshevism'. During the afternoon of the 20th, Hitler accepted congratulations in the *Fuhrerbunker*. For the last time most of the big names, Himmler, Göring, Ribbentrop, Speer and Dönitz were there, as were also, of course, Goebbels, Bormann, Keitel, Jodl, and Krebs. Mussolini sent good wishes by telegram. Hitler was confident and affable. He predicted that the Russians would suffer their bloodiest defeat before Berlin; and he shook hands and spoke with everyone.

One of those present was Colonel-General Karl Koller, the Luftwaffe Chief-of-Staff, sombre and conscientious. When the afternoon situation conference finally began, he announced that the roads out of Berlin to the south would not stay open much longer. Those who were going to the southern command post would have to leave that night by automobile. The Luftwaffe did not have planes to fly them out; besides, it was too dangerous. The birthday celebration therewith also became the time of parting. All of those who stood high enough to venture unsolicited advice urged Hitler to leave the city too. Hitler declined to go, indicating he wanted more time to make up his mind.

He must have known that from the purely technical point of view it would soon become most difficult, if not impossible, to conduct the war from Berlin. The Russians were drawing close to the army communications centre at Zossen and could be there almost any hour. The only comparable installation in Germany was the one in the Berghof complex outside Berchtesgaden in the Bavarian Alps. There, throughout the war, Hitler had vacationed every year with Eva Braun – usually in March and April as a matter of fact – and an elaborate communications system had been set up for his use at those times. The Berghof and the installations at the foot of the Obersalzberg were still intact, protected from Allied planes by batteries of smoke generators. Hitler had indicated late in March that he regarded them as the best

Soviet bombers over Berlin

alternative command post if Zossen were bombed out or lost.

During the night on the 20th General August Winter, Jodl's deputy, who was to be chief of staff of Command Staff B (the southern command), departed in a truck and automobile convoy with most of the essential personnel of the Armed Forces Operations Staff and the Army Operations Branch. Göring, also going south, left after midnight, having had to take cover for several hours in the public air raid shelters in Berlin, where he had a last opportunity to wring some laughs out of his old joke stemming from a speech he had made early in the war in which he had told the Germans they could 'call me Meyer if the Allies ever bomb Berlin'. People in nearby shelters had invited him to visit them too, and he had. As a result, it was half past two before his car, tyres screeching, rolled into the Luftwaffe headquarters compound at Wildpark-Werder. Half an hour later, after collecting a column of vehicles, he roared through the gate at high speed without having troubled to say goodbye to or leave orders for his chief-of-staff, Koller.

Others also left Berlin that night. In the afternoon Hitler had given

Dönitz full authority over material and manpower in the northern area – but not tactical command. Dönitz went out to establish Command Staff A at Plon in Schleswig, south of Kiel. Himmler was another who left. He would be in Hohenlychen the next morning talking to Count Bernadotte of the Swedish Red Cross about negotiating a separate armistice with the British and Americans.

Koller had barely had time to rest a few hours after watching his chief's unceremonious departure when he was summoned to the telephone. It was Hitler wanting to know whether Koller heard the artillery shells exploding in Berlin. Koller explained that he could hardly be expected to hear them where he was in the western suburbs. Hitler insisted it must be railway guns the Russians were using and that meant they must have built a bridge across the Oder. Actually, Russian artillery had been firing into parts of Berlin since the 19th, only not into the centre of the city where Hitler was. Koller had a minor inspiration. He called the Flak tower in the Tiergarten, not far from the *Fuhrerbunker*. From their hundred-foot high concrete gun platform the anti-aircraft crews could see across almost the entire city now that the buildings roundabout were pretty well leveled

When their buildings were destroyed, hospitals moved into the streets

by the bombing. The crews in the Flak tower reported that they had seen the Russian guns go into position after daylight that morning about seven miles from the centre of Berlin. (The distance must have been some miles greater since the Russians were not yet inside the Berlin outer defence ring.) The guns were 100-mm, 120-mm at most. The Flak tower's own 128-mm twin anti-aircraft guns were firing back. Hitler refused to believe it when Koller told him.

In the *Fuhrerbunker* the day brought a glimmer of good news: IV Panzer Army was having some local success in a counterattack northwest of Görlitz. Hitler saw in it the makings of a major thrust that would close the forty mile gap between the Army Group Vistula-Army Group Centre flanks, and from that illusion he derived a 'basic order' which Krebs transmitted to Army Group Vistula by phone in the afternoon. The 'successful' attack at Army Group Centre would soon close the front at Spremberg; therefore, it was 'absolutely necessary' to hold the corner post at Cottbus. (The day before, IX Army had taken command of IV Panzer Army's left flank corps which was at Cottbus

on the north side of the gap.) The IX Army would set up a front facing west between Königswusterhausen and Cottbus and attack west into the flank of the Russians going towards Berlin from the south. Steiner would command an operation to close the front north of Berlin on the line of the Berlin Stettin *Autobahn*. The III Panzer Army would eliminate 'every last bridgehead on the Oder' and get ready to attack south. Reymann, relieved as Berlin commandant, would command on the front south of Berlin.

At first nobody knew just where Steiner was. His services had been in small demand since the Stargard offensive. As a result, Koller went through his second nervous ordeal of the day. Hitler called to demand that all the Luftwaffe troops fit for ground combat, including 'a division' he claimed Göring had been keeping as a personal guard at Karinhall, be sent to Steiner immediately. Koller could not find anyone who could tell him where Steiner might be. Heinrici had given Steiner's III SS Panzer Corps head-quarters, which so far had no troops of its own, the task of scraping up enough to set up a screening line on III Panzer Army's south flank along the Finow Canal.

In the order that went out to Steiner in the late afternoon, Hitler elevated

Steiner's command to an *Armee-abteilung* (an 'army detachment' – more than a corps but not quite an army) and gave him the IV SS Police Division, V Jäger Division, and XXV Panzer Grenadier Division, all north of the Finow Canal, and the LVI Panzer Corps, then still standing east of Berlin with its north flank just below Wreneuchen. With the three divisions, Steiner was to attack south from Eberswalde on the canal, 15 miles north of Berlin, to the LVI Panzer Corps flank and close the front. To the tactical directive Hitler added, 'Officers who do not accept this order without reservation are to be arrested and shot instantly. You yourself I make responsible with your head for its execution.' Hitler was trying to make terror a tool of command. In his exchanges with Koller he declared that any commander who had orders to send troops to Steiner and held them back would be a dead man 'within five hours'.

As soon as he received the order Steiner called the army group headquarters to report that it could not be carried out. Only two battalions of the IV SS Police Division were at hand, and they were not armed for combat. The V Jäger and XXV Panzer Grenadier Divisions were tied down in the front and could not be used until the II Naval Division arrived from the coast to relieve them.

When Krebs phoned a resumé of the Steiner order to the army group headquarters, Heinrici asked him to impress on Hitler the necessity for taking back IX Army, which was being encircled and even then could no longer withdraw towards Berlin but would have to go around the lake chain south of the city. If Hitler insisted on keeping his previous orders in force, then Heinrici asked to be relieved because he could not execute them and he could not reconcile them with his conscience and his responsibility to the troops. Krebs answered that the Führer took responsibility for his own orders.

During the day on the 21st, 2nd Guards Tank Army advanced nearly thirty miles north of Berlin, and an attack southwest of Werneuchen carried to the Berlin outer defence ring. North of Müggel Lake, in the south-eastern suburbs, the 1st Guards Tank and 8th Guards Armies also reached the outer defence ring. The IX Army observed a strong build-up on its north flank between Müggel Lake and Fürstenwalde, but the Russians did not on that day continue the attack south-west to cut the army off from the city. Behind IX Army the point of 3rd Guards Tank Army reached Königswusterhausen, five miles south of Berlin.

The Soviet command decision on the 21st was intended, first, to accomplish the encirclement of Berlin and, in the second order of business, to envelop IX Army. North of the capital, the two armies assigned the flank thrust were finally making enough speed to take over their screening mission, and Sokolovsky ordered the 2nd Guards Tank and 47th Armies to concentrate on completing the encirclement. Approaching Berlin, 1st Guards Tank and 8th Guards Armies had slowed down and then come almost to a stop on the outer defence ring, which delayed the envelopment of IX Army south-west of the line Müggel Lake/Fürstenwalde. The Russian troops were clearly not in the mood to garner last-minute laurels. The 1st Belorussian Front's two-army force in the Frankfurt bridgehead had not accomplished anything. By the 21st its mission had become superfluous, and it was, therefore, assigned to assist in the encirclement of IX Army. The 3rd Guards Tank and 13 Armies' rapid advance had stretched thin the enveloping front behind IX Army and had tended to draw the two Soviet armies east. On the 21st Konev put in 28th Army from his reserve to take over part of the front against IX Army and free the 3rd Guards Tank and 13th Armies to close in on Berlin from the south while 4th Guards Tank Army attacked towards Potsdam.

At one o'clock in the afternoon of the 22nd, Koller's phone to the *Fuhrerbunker* rang again. It was the Luftwaffe liaison officer, General Eckhardt Christian. Hitler wanted to know whether Steiner had attacked. Koller had troubles enough of his own. During the night the German line had moved north-west behind the Havel River, and Koller's headquarters was now on the enemy side of the front.

Even amid the ruins, the Germans find time for a parade

Koller, who still had the use of the extensive Luftwaffe telephone network, made some calls and soon learned that Steiner was 'getting ready' but had not attacked. When he reported that back to the *Fuhrerbunker* he brought down on himself a deluge of arguments and questions. The army had reported that Steiner had attacked. Himmler 'was positive' Steiner had attacked. Why could not the Luftwaffe send out a plane to see what actually was happening? Koller – 'because the pilot would not know where to look and could not see anything in the smoke and dust anyway'. At half past five Koller called the *Fuhrerbunker* to say he would come there to report in person. Christian told him it was not necessary any more; historic events were in the making, the decisive ones for the whole war. He would come to Werder to give a report on them.

At the afternoon situation conference Hitler had broken down. When, having waited impatiently through the morning and early afternoon for a report from Steiner, he at last became convinced that Steiner had not attacked, he fell into a tearful rage, declared the war was lost, blamed it all on the generals, and announced that he would stay in Berlin to the end and kill himself before the Russians could take him prisoner. He ordered his papers and records taken out and burned. Goebbels swore he would stay to the end, and with his wife and six children moved into the *Vorbunker*, taking the rooms Morell had left the day before, after Hitler had accused him of trying to give him morphine and dismissed him. Bormann, Keitel, and Jodl tried to persuade Hitler to go out of Berlin because it was impossible to exercise command from there any more. When he refused, Keitel and Jodl declined an order to fly out to the southern command post and pledged themselves to stand by him.

As had happened many times before, the emotional storm passed quickly. The 'historic events' Christian had predicted were not quite ready to come yet. Jodl remembered that they had Wenck's XII Army on the front facing the Americans south-east of Magdeburg. He remembered, too, from the captured Eclipse order, that the British and Americans were already well into the Russian zone and, therefore, probably would not go beyond the Elbe. Hitler first rejected as a waste of time Jodl's suggestion that they turn XII Army around and have it attack east. Then, in a few minutes, he took up the idea and was off on another round of planning.

During his breakdown, Hitler had finally admitted that the régime was utterly bankrupt. For him and his associates all that was left was the consolation they could draw from keeping the machinery running a

Overleaf: **For civilian and military alike, the future looked bleak.** *Above right:* **Fire-fighting squads.** *Below right:* **The refugees leave their city**

while longer even though it would accomplish nothing. Keitel was the outstanding example. Filled with purposeless dedication, he took on himself the role of field-marshal/messenger and set out to carry the turnaround order to Wenck, a task that could be and, in fact, was, accomplished far more quickly by telephone.

Before the conference ended, Krebs was on the phone to Heinrici telling him the Führer was making the decision; Schörner and Wenck would be briefed; Wenck would attack east; Schörner's attack east of Bautzen was succeeding; IX Army would have to hold Cottbus and the Oder line to the south of Frankfurt. In short, Hitler was back at trying to build a front east of Berlin.

Reports coming in from the front revealed how slim the chances were. Steiner called the army group after dark to say he had not been able to attack because his troops were not assembled which everybody knew by then. Heinrici told him to attack that night, ready or not. Against III Panzer Army, 2nd Belorussian Front had, by nightfall, taken a bridgehead 10 miles long upstream from Stettin. The IX Army had lost Cottbus during the day and was broken through south of Frankfurt. North of Berlin, Russian tank spearheads were on the Havel river; and on the east, the Russians had at one point penetrated the inner defence ring.

But when Krebs called Heinrici again at nine o'clock, he was full of optimism. The Wenck attack would bring relief fast, he said; one division would attack that night. Heinrici disagreed. Wenck, he objected, had a long way to go. Heinrici wanted at least to take IV Army back twenty miles or so, out of the bulge on the Oder upstream from Frankfurt. 'Tell the Führer', he added, 'I do this not because I am against him but because I am for him'. Finally, at midnight, Heinrici received permission to let IX Army withdraw to a line from north of Cottbus to Lieberose, and the Spree. In doing so Busse was to free a division for a thrust west to meet XII Army.

The next day, the 23rd, the encirclement of Berlin entered its last stage. The 1st Belorussian Front committed its second echelon, 3rd Army, to cut

the narrow corridor connecting IX Army with Berlin. From the south the 3rd Guards Tank and 13th Armies closed to the outer defence ring, and 4th Guards Tank Army approached Potsdam. North of Berlin, 3nd Guards Tank Army crossed the Havel below Oranienburg and began turning south. In the city that afternoon Hitler held his last big situation conference. When it broke up, Keitel went out to bring his 'personal influence' to bear on XII Army, and Jodl headed north with what was left of the Armed Forces Operations Staff to Neu Roofen, behind III Panzer Army.

In the afternoon Hitler ordered General Helmuth Weidling, Commanding General, LVI Panzer Corps, to take over with his troops, which Busse had wanted to use to protect IX Army's north flank, the eastern and southeastern defences of the city. Hitler later also made Weidling, whom he had only the day before intended to have shot for disobeying orders, defence commandant of all Berlin. When Krebs told him of the appointment, Weidling said he would rather they had shot him. Weidling, who had begun his military career in 1911 as an enlisted man, arrived late and, by his own account, reluctantly on the centre of the historical stage. Nevertheless, the next few days would cost him ten years of his life. He died in 1955, a prisoner of the Russians.

After the situation conference, Heinrici received a telephone order to stop the Steiner attack 'at once', give up the Eberswalde bridgehead, and shift Steiner's headquarters and troops twenty five miles west to Oranienburg for a thrust into the flank of the Russians crossing the Havel. The order added that XII Army was sending XXXXI Panzer to hem in the Russians from the west. Steiner had made a little progress south of Eberswalde early in the day but far less than enough to have any effect.

By the end of the day, Hitler, through his order pulling LVI Panzer Corps into Berlin, had made it a certainty that IX Army would soon be completely isolated and encircled. When Heinrici talked to Busse that night, after the telephone connections had been out all day, Busse reported that they would have to make the

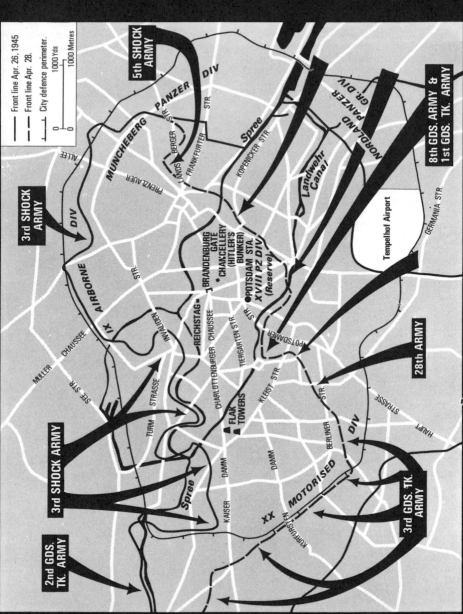

The Russian thrusts into the heart of the city

breakout to the west – if one were to be made – with small arms since his artillery ammunition was exhausted. His north front, he said, was disintegrating because it was losing the support it had been getting from Berlin. He summed up his predicament in a sentence, 'I was kept forward too long' Heinrici replied, 'That was a crime'. When they finished Heinrici called Wenck and told him he must rescue his 'old friend', Busse.

On the 24th the Russians worked systematically to complete the great circle of steel and fire around Berlin. Eight armies, four of them tank armies, were closing in on the city. The battle was lost; it would have been given up but for one man, who, prematurely aged, palsied, and buried under six yards of earth and concrete out of sight and hearing of the destruction rolling in on him, demanded and got absolute obedience.

Berlin was no Stalingrad. It might hold out, through fanaticism and terror, for a few days, no more. On the north and east the Russians were approaching the S-Bahn defence ring, the last outside city centre. During the day 1st Belorussian and 1st Ukrainian Fronts' forces met at Bohnsdorf to close the encirclement of the southeast and isolate IX Army. The 4th Guards Tank Army reached the lakes flanking Potsdam and 2nd Guards Tank Army, coming from the north, went as far as Nauen and south almost to Spandau. The Havel bridges at Spandau were the last exits to the west still open. In the city, LVI Panzer Corps occupied the south-east sector; the rest of the sectors were held by *Volkssturm*, SS, and Hitler Jugend formations. The four massive Flak towers stood like stranded concrete battleships, powerful and helpless. Weidling discovered to his horror that his predecessors had tried to exercise command through the public telephone system.

Hitler, deprived of all but the last remnants of his once elaborate command apparatus, nevertheless ordered, 'The Armed Forces High Command . . . will command in accordance with my directives which I will transmit through the Chief-of-Staff, Army, who is with me'. He terminated the Army General Staff command functions and

undertook to exercise control on the north directly through the Armed Forces Operations Staff, and in the south more loosely through the Command Staff B and the army groups. For the south he issued a half hearted directive to create, as far as that could still be accomplished, a redoubt in the Alps. His conception of how it should be done did not go much beyond the general statement that it was to be 'envisioned as the final bulwark of fanatical resistance and so prepared'. For him the war had narrowed down to Berlin. He established as the 'main mission' of the Armed Forces High Command to attack from the north-west, south-west, and south to regain contact with Berlin and 'so decide the battle for the capital victoriously'.

In Jodl and Keitel, Hitler had ideal collaborators in futility. Neither gave a thought to anything beyond getting through to the Führer, above all not to question, WHY? Before the day was out Jodl had changed the directions of the IX and XII Armies: one was to attack north-west, the other north-east toward Berlin.

On 25th April the Soviet spearheads met north-west of Potsdam. On the Elbe, sixty miles south-west of Berlin, the US 1st Army and Soviet 5th Guards Army made contact at Torgau. In an order to Dönitz, Hitler described the fighting around Berlin as the 'battle for the German fate', all other fronts and all other missions henceforth being secondary. He instructed the Admiral to send reinforcements to Berlin by air and to the fronts around the city by 'land and by sea'. The Armed Forces High Command had already directed the theatre commanders to regard the conflict with the Soviet forces as paramount and to accept 'greater losses to the Anglo-Americans' for the sake of releasing units to be committed against the Russians.

To the extent that the German fate still remained to be decided, however, the day's most significant development was neither at Berlin nor on the Elbe but on the Oder, where Rokossovsky's 2nd Belorussian Front broke the III Panzer Army's line around the bridgehead south of Stettin and crossed the Randow Swamp toward Prenzlau.

No relief

The 25th April communiqué on the war sent out to the few newspapers still publishing in Germany described Hitler as 'personally making the decisions on deployment of forces and calling in of reinforcements in the defence of the capital of the Reich against the Bolshevik assault'. It added, as if that were a desirable innovation, that Hitler was now himself awarding medals immediately after the action in which they had been earned. As far as it went, the communiqué was factual. Hitler *was* in command of the battle for Berlin, and he *was* awarding medals at an unparalleled rate, many – perhaps most of them – to Hitler Jugend brought in by the Reich Youth Leader, Arthur Axmann, who was still in regular attendance at the *Fuhrerbunker*. The Russians later found a closetful of medals in the Chancellory, enough for several more years of war.

Half an hour after midnight on the 25th a directive Hitler had written the evening before reached the Armed Forces High Command headquarters at Neu Roofen. It called for the 'fastest execution of all relief attacks, without regard for flanks and neighbours'. Although he must have known his time was running pitifully short, Hitler still insisted on attempting nothing less than to restore a complete and solid front on the east. The XII Army was to strike north-east from Belzig to Ferch at the tip of the twin lakes south of Potsdam while IX Army attacked west to meet it. After they had joined, both armies were to advance toward Berlin from the south 'on a broad front'. The IX Army, meanwhile, was also to hold its eastern front so that Army Group Centre could close up from the south. Steiner was to attack toward Berlin from north-west of Oranienburg with the XXV Panzer Grenadier Division, the II Naval Division, and the VII Panzer Division. The III Panzer Army was to 'prevent an expansion of the Oder bridgehead'.

Jodl answered that all the relief movements had begun or were about to begin. He also called attention to the 2nd Belorussian Front threat east of Prenzlau and to a 21st Army Group (British) build-up south-east of Hamburg that indicated a thrust toward Lubeck. (Montgomery was preparing the drive across the Elbe to the Baltic coast that Eisenhower had promised him.) To counter those, Jodl proposed withdrawing the German forces on the North Sea coast west of the Elbe.

Day dawned bright and clear on the 26th. The battle was being fought in ideal spring weather, and that day

Russians ride their tanks into Berlin

Street fighting in the suburbs. Russian soldiers advance

sunshine and a whiff of fresh air seemed almost to have penetrated smoke, dust, and concrete and entered the *Fuhrerbunker*. Weidling remembered it as the 'day of hopes'; Krebs repeatedly phoned him in his command post on the Bendlerstrasse to announce good news. The naval liaison officer's morning report to Dönitz reflected the interpretation being put on Jodl's message in the *Fuhrerbunker*: IX and XII Armies were having 'gratifying successes'; Steiner was 'making progress'; and Schörner's attack at Bautzen showed that 'when the will is there, the enemy can be defeated even today'. Hitler's resurgent confidence found expression in his reply to Jodl' He wanted the Elbe line held against Montgomery and the 'bridgehead' east of Prenzlau not only contained but reduced. He did not object to taking forces from west of the Elbe, but it was to be done without losing the ports, Emden, Wilhelms-haven, and Wesermunde, or losing the use of the Kaiser Wilhelm (Kiel) Canal.

In the evening the telephone lines to Berlin went dead, and communication with the pocket was shifted to line of sight short-wave, transmitted from a balloon run up near the Armed Forces High Command headquarters. In a mood of self-immolation, Jodl and Keitel intended to fly into the pocket that night for one more situation conference, but the landing strip in the Tiergarten was closed by smoke, shell holes, and wrecked aircraft. The last to land that night were Colonel-General Robert Ritter von Greim and Hanna Reitsch, a daredevil woman test pilot.

Hitler had summoned Greim, an old associate from the early days of the Nazi movement, to Berlin from Munich to resolve a command crisis in the Luftwaffe. On the 23rd, after talking to Christian and, briefly, to Jodl, Koller had flown south to Command Post B. There he had given Göring a report on Hitler's breakdown, including a statement Hitler had made that there was not much left to fight for and if it came to negotiating, Göring could do that better than he. Koller either was not aware of or failed to report Hitler's recovery, and Göring had immediately sent off a telegram asking whether he, as the

Russians in action with Katyusha rocket mortar batteries

Führer's deputy, should take over leadership of the Reich 'including complete freedom of negotiation'. In the reply drafted by Bormann, no doubt with considerable relish, Hitler had dismissed Göring from all his official posts, 'including that of Reich Chief Hunter'. In a telegram to the SS guard at Berchstesgaden Hitler had ordered Göring's arrest with the provision that his life be spared as a mark of 'the Führer's generosity'. In the *Fuhrerbunker* on the night of the 26th, Hitler named Greim to replace Göring as Commander in Chief, Luftwaffe, and promoted him to field-marshal.

Outside the Berlin pocket, during the day on the 26th the German commands launched into the pursuit of two incompatible and, considering the state of the German forces, mutually exclusive objectives: Heinrici became intent on holding together what was left of his front and rescuing IX Army, while Keitel and Jodl concentrated entirely on the Berlin relief. Heinrici wanted to save what could still be saved. Keitel and Jodl tried once more to force reality to bend to the Führer's will. To them this was nothing new. They had watched him sacrifice armies in an almost unbroken succession of similar attempts since Stalingrad. It was the essence of the Führer Principle, it was Hitler's formula for victory; and it had one fault – it never worked.

Steiner had advanced and taken a small bridgehead on the Havel west of Oranienburg during the night, but after daylight he was stopped. All he had was the XXV Panzer Grenadier Division. The II Naval Division was strung out on the railroads between Oranienburg and the coast, and the VII Panzer Division, brought into Swinemünde by sea from Danzig only days before, had no vehicles with which to move out of its assembly area west of Neubrandenburg. Before noon on the 26th, Heinrici proposed giving up the Steiner attack because it could not be expected to succeed. He wanted to use the divisions against the Soviet breakthrough east of Prenzlau. Jodl refused.

By late afternoon 2nd Belorussian Front had chewed through III Panzer Army's last reserves and was approaching Penzlau. General Hasso von Manteuffel, commanding III Panzer

Orderly withdrawal for female troops

KAPITULIEREN ? NEIN

Left: Russian mortar section. *Above:* Surrender? No! *Below:* Veteran and young recruit wait for the tanks with their Panzerfaust, German 'bazooka'

Army, was withdrawing on his flanks to get troops to put into the gap opening in his centre. Heinrici concluded that a decision had to be made concerning Steiner; his operation could not influence the fate of Berlin and was tying down the army group's 'last and only' motorised division. The question was, where could the decision come from? By direct interference, Jodl and Keitel had practically removed Steiner from Heinrici's command.

The XII Army, the mainstay of the relief operation, did not expect to accomplish more than to get a wedge through that would allow the Berlin civilians and garrison to escape. After several changes, its assigned missions were to assist the Steiner operation from the west with XXXXI Panzer Corps, cover the Elbe line and defend Brandenburg, and advance northeast from Belzig toward Berlin. In other words, the army was in the peculiar position of having to defend on the west while attacking to the east. On the 26th, XX Corps, the Berlin relief corps, was fully occupied with defending the line Brandenburg/Belzig/Wittenberg to protect its staging area

Mopping up street resistance

against the Americans.

The IX Army began its breakout attempt on the 26th with a thrust to the Baruth – Zossen section of the Berlin/Dresden *Autobahn*. The army's strength was sinking fast. The night before, all the promised air supply had been diverted to Berlin. Jodl, after his last telephone conversation with Hitler, was still determined to 'make clear to IX Army that it must turn sharply [north] together with XII Army to relieve Berlin.' Jodl and Heinrici argued over where the day's air supply, such as it might be, should go. Heinrici maintained that IX Army deserved the aid because the high commands were responsible for its being where it was. Jodl insisted that the people of Berlin and the 'Head of

State' could not be left in the lurch and suggested that any thought to the contrary was treason. Off IX Army's south flank, Schörner's drive, having made about fifteen miles in six days, was close to a standstill with forty miles yet to go.

During the night of the 26th, III Panzer Army withdrew to the Ucker River and the line of lakes south of Prenzlau. It was the army's last chance to keep from being overrun, and it failed. In the morning Rokossovsky's tanks drove past Penzlau and his infantry streamed into the gap behind them. In the afternoon Heinrici sent his chief of staff to Dönitz's headquarters to report to the Admiral that the army group was defeated, and was retreating west through Mecklenburg.

If Heinrici expected a decision from

though less ostentatiously, he counted himself among Hitler's paladins as much as did Jodl and Keitel.

The Armed Forces High Command, marking time on 27th April, issued orders in all directions. To stop the Russians west of Prenzlau, Headquarters, 21 Army (the former 4th Army Staff), under General Kurt von Tippelskirch, was to be put in with two regiments, neither of them to be available for at least another twenty four hours. Hitler had lost faith in Steiner, and an order went out for XXXXI Panzer Corps to take command of the Oranienburg attack, but the corps headquarters reported that it was too far away to assume effective control. Hitler had called on the IX and XII Armies to do their duty, to unite and attack toward Berlin, and so attain 'the decisive turning point of the war'. Transmitting Hitler's message to the armies, Keitel added, 'History and the German people will despise everyone who does not do his utmost to save the situation and the Führer'. Keitel directed Schörner, in case contact with the Armed Forces High Command was lost, to keep on attacking north from Bautzen toward the IX and XII Armies.

Late in the afternoon Jodl at last concluded, 'The enemy clearly has broken through III Panzer Army at Prenzlau.' He decided, 'onerous as it is', to stop the Steiner attack; but he could not, even yet, bring himself to give it up entirely. The order to Heinrici stated that he could have the XXV Panzer Grenadier Division and the VII Panzer Division for a counter-attack into the Russian flank from the southwest. Afterwards the divisions were to be turned south towards Berlin again.

An hour and a half before midnight Manteuffel called the army group and reported that half of his divisions and the entire Flak artillery had stopped fighting. A hundred thousand men were fleeing west. He had not seen anything like it, he said, even in 1918; it would take hundreds of officers to stop them. The war was over, he added; the soldiers had 'spoken'; some

Dönitz, he was bound to be disappointed. At a situation conference several hours before – at which Dönitz and Himmler, to their mutual chagrin, both insisted on receiving Keitel's and Jodl's reports seated as was Hitler's custom – it had been decided that Dönitz would not exercise military command until it became impossible for the Army Forces High Command to secure orders from Hitler. In any event, not much was to be expected of Dönitz's military judgment; he had lately begun to quibble about holding Stettin and Swinemünde, where III Panzer Army's north flank was in imminent danger of being trapped, so that the Navy could keep contact with Army Group Courland. Dönitz might have stretched his civil powers to include negotiating a surrender; but he was not the man for that;

Overleaf, above: A few found transport to leave the city. *Below:* Most had to walk. *Right:* And many, old and young, simply waited for a train

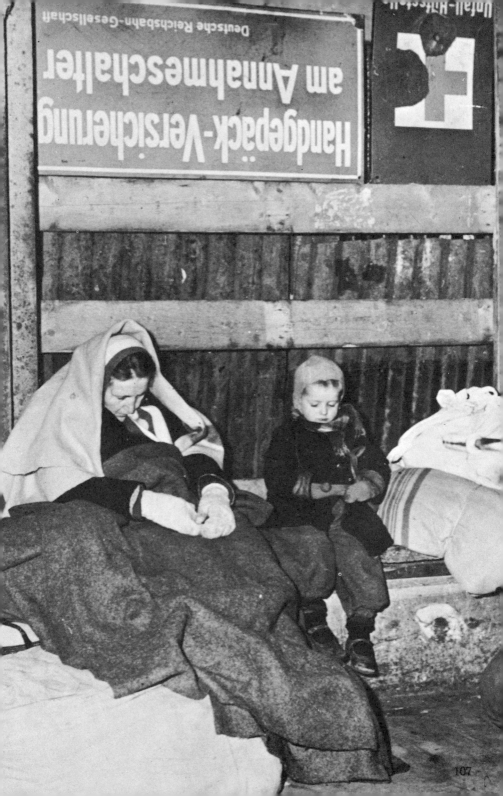

Soviet soldiers storm the Reichstag.
And hoist their flag on its roof.
They fire a salvo in triumph

of the officers would stand and let themselves be shot, but that would not accomplish anything. He proposed sending Jodl out to see for himself what a waste of time it was to talk about relieving Berlin. All that was left was to negotiate, preferably with the Western Allies, and meanwhile retreat west fast enough to hold the remnants of the army together.

In the morning Keitel set out toward the front intending to lend the stimulus of his presence to the preparations for the counterattack on the III Panzer Army flank. At Zehdenick on the Havel, to his huge astonishment and dismay, he encountered a rear party of the V Jäger Division surveying a defence line on the river. He had thought the front was twenty miles farther east and, complying with his orders, would stay there. Subsequently he also learned that the counterattack would not be made from Templin as had been ordered. Heinrici and Manteuffel had decided the evening before that the VII Panzer Division and XXV Panzer Grenadier Division could not be deployed there in time and, therefore, should be put in farther north, east of Neubrandenburg and Neustrelitz, to oppose the Russians frontally. That, of course, as Keitel was fully aware, also took the two divisions farther away from Berlin.

In the afternoon Keitel met with Heinrici and Manteuffel. By then Jodl had phoned Heinrici talking of treason and threatening the 'ultimate consequences' if Heinrici did not execute orders as they were given. In what Heinrici described later as a 'colossal discussion' and an 'atrocious development', Keitel ordered the two generals to stand and to counterattack south-east of Neustrelitz.

Keitel gave the order to stand in the midst of a front that was disintegrating all around him – Heinrici took three hours covering twenty or so miles back to his headquarters. The roads were clogged with refugees and retreating troops; Neubrandenburg was completely blocked. The troops, Heinrici observed, were 'marching home in columns'.

The troops would not stand, and nothing could make them do so. Heinrici called Keitel at midnight to tell him that the Russians were on the Havel on III Panzer Army's south flank. When Keitel replied that that was what happened 'if one gives up positions voluntarily', Heinrici protested that he had been deprived of authority to make decisions within his own command. Keitel answered that it had been necessary because the Führer's orders were not being carried out and therewith relieved Heinrici, ordering him to turn over the command to Manteuffel as the senior army commander.

The day dawned on the 28th on a tormented city and a dying war. Keitel kept alive the fiction of an attack from Oranienburg, but the only relief operation with any prospect of being executed was Wenck's. The IX Army's breakout failed during the day. The tank point in the lead became separated and was not heard from again. Konstantin Simonov, the famous Russian novelist, then like most other Soviet literary figures a war correspondent, drove along the Baruth/Zossen stretch of the *Autobahn* several days later on his way from Torgau to Berlin. He described the road as littered for miles on either side with wrecked tanks and trucks and with dead and wounded that the Russians had not had time to move. Busse reported that IX Army was neither in condition to make a concerted second attempt to get out of the pocket nor in condition to hold out much longer.

In Berlin the eight Soviet armies that had closed in on the city had begun attacking through the S-Bahn ring on the 26th, after heavy bombings during the previous day and night. By nightfall on the 27th the Russians had cut off Reymann's force in Potsdam and pushed the Berlin defenders into a pocket nine and a half miles long from east and west and from one to three miles wide. On the west the pocket still reached nearly to the Havel river, but the Russians held the crossings. In the centre of the city, the Russians had driven spearheads through from the north and south to the edges of the government quarter and the Soviet armies were competing for the honor of taking the Reichstag – which to the Russians, even though it had been a charred ruin since 1933, had come to symbolize the Third Reich.

Into the abyss

The battle for Berlin was fought outside the city; what went on in the capital was hardly more than a contested mop-up. The fortress had never come into existence. When SS General Gustav Krukenberg came into Berlin on 24th April to take command of the SS 'Nordland' Division, he found the Havel bridges at Spandau barricaded but not defended. From there he drove through all of West Berlin 'without encountering soldiers or defence installations of any kind'. In the *Fuhrerbunker*, Krebs told him that the ninety volunteers from the 'Charlemagne' Division Krukenberg had brought with him were the only ones who had arrived of numerous officers and troop units ordered into Berlin. The 'Nordland' Division, Krukenberg discovered, had the strength of about a battalion. Three days later, when he became a sector commander in the centre of the city, his command post was a subway car without either a telephone or lights. The fighting in Berlin lasted as long as it did because a great metropolis, bombed out though it might be and no matter how amateurishly fortified, cannot be taken quickly, even against a lame defence, particularly not by troops who know the war is over and intend to see their homes again.

Berlin did not go down, as Hitler had imagined, in a Wagnerian burst of glory but in a ragged wave of destruction and despair. Corpses hanging in the streets, the work of single-officer flying courts martial that passed only death sentences, showed soldiers and civilians what they could expect of their own leadership. But that leadership was operating on residual momentum; it could no longer formulate, deliver, or enforce purposeful orders. Individuals might be hanged; whole units could hide out. With rockets and artillery, the Russians evened the scores for Leningrad and Stalingrad as far as they could. But in the air raid shelters where Berlin life had centred for months, Soviet shells and rockets had nowhere near the effect Allied bombs had had, nor did they in the long run add greatly to the damage already inflicted on the city.

War, however, does not have to make sense and battles do not have to be decisive to be terrible. As an example of the horror and human destruction that can be accomplished by modern warfare Berlin undoubtedly ranks along with Leningrad, Kharkov, Budapest, Dresden, Hamburg, Hiroshima, Nagasaki, and the dozens of other cities that suffered in numbers and in a manner not seen since the Thirty

Some of the thousands who died fighting

With carts and cars and bicycles, the endless trek goes on

Years' War. Whether the work of starvation and cold in Leningrad, or of fire bombs on Dresden and Hamburg, or of the atom at Nagasaki and Hiroshima constituted the ultimate expression of war's frightfulness may be pointless to argue. Nevertheless, it is a fact that the Second World War singled out certain cities for distinct, specialised tortures. For Berlin, it was the fighting of a house-to-house, street-to-street battle in a city crowded with civilians. Although the population was considerably below its normal number, the one and three-quarter million people still there were more than the city could accommodate or care for even before the battle began. Moreover, the overwhelming majority of the civilians were women and children and the aged. The troops had at least one thing in common with the highest command, they were part of the apparatus, and while it functioned they could imagine it did so to some purpose. The civilians had to fend entirely for themselves.

The Panzer Division 'Müncheberg', one of the divisions in Weidling's corps, held Sector D, almost due south of the Reich Chancellory. On 26th April its front was on the Tempelhof Airfield just inside the S-Bahn ring and about four miles away from the Chancellory. The division had a dozen tanks and thirty armoured personnel carriers. It was to have received infantry reinforcements. What it got were *Volkssturm* men and stragglers. In the rear civilians, carrying what they could of their possessions, were moving deeper into the city. The division's wounded stayed at the front, afraid of being picked up by the flying courts martial and hanged as deserters if they left.

Smoke and the fumes of burned explosives were everywhere. The dead lay in the streets where they had been felled by artillery shells or exploding rockets. Many of them were women with a bucket or pot of some kind still in their hand or nearby. They had come out of the cellars for water. The Russians were approaching cautiously through the built-up district south of the airfield, burning their way into buildings with flame-throwers as they came. In the brief intervals of quiet, the screams of women and children reached the division's line.

At dusk, Russian tanks carrying infantry rolled across the airfield. The line held through the night, but after daylight the tanks came on in waves. In the afternoon on the 27th the division began to go back. It would not be able to come to a stop anywhere again for more than a few hours. Behind it, civilians fled from cellar to

cellar. On walls and sidewalks slogans were scrawled in foot-high letters – 'It is darkest before dawn' – 'We retreat, but we will win'. For those who might not draw inspiration from such philosophical exhortations there were more graphic displays, the bodies of 'deserters' who had been shot or hanged, each with a placard around his neck stating his offence.

From the south, east, and north the defenders were driven back into the center of the city. On the 28th, the 'Müncheberg' Division set up in and around the Anhalter Station, less than half a mile south of the Reich Chancellory. Krukenberg's 'Nordland' Division was there too. The underground platforms were crowded with women

Overleaf: The innumerable victims of an air raid. *Above right:* A casualty is hurried to cover. *Below:* Russian artillery detachment

115

and children, military command posts, and wounded, all listening anxiously to the noise of battle overhead and trying to avoid the falling chunks of concrete chipped out of the tunnel ceilings by shells impacting on the streets above. Occasional trains rolled slowly through, going nobody knew where.

Suddenly, water flowed into the tunnels, rising in a few minutes to a depth of a yard or more and touching off a panic in which wounded and children were forgotten in the rush to get above ground. Allegedly on orders from Hitler, who wanted to keep the Russians from advancing through them, engineers had blown the bulkheads that separated the tunnels from the nearby Landwehr Canal. Later it was reported that thousands drowned in the tunnels that day, but, actually, after the first flood the water subsided and the tunnels then filled up gradually. No doubt some were trampled in the panic and some drowned, but the official who was in charge of pumping out the subways in October 1945 has stated that most of the bodies found in the tunnels were apparently those of persons who had died of wounds before being placed there.

The 'Müncheberg' Division was forced to retreat north-west to the Potsdamer Station in the afternoon on the 28th. Then it was just around the corner from the Riech Chancellory. The main entrance to the station presented a gruesome sight. A heavy explosion in the corridor had literally plastered men, women and children against the walls. Outside, the Potsdamer Platz was littered with smashed vehicles, ambulances with the wounded still lying in them, and corpses run over by trucks and tanks and horribly mutilated. Civilians were refusing to let wounded into the cellars for fear of being tried themselves by the flying courts martial as accomplices in desertion. The troops were tired, hungry, desperate. During the night, artillery fire rained on the centre of the city heavier than before, and the Russians began pushing towards the station through the subway tunnels.

Hitler did not concern himself with the human aspect of the fighting in Berlin any more than he had when the front was deep in Russia. The concrete of the *Fuhrerbunker* and the steady roar of the diesel-driven ventilating system provided almost perfect insulation against the sight and sound; nevertheless, occasionally, shell explosions close by shook the bunker and the ventilators drew in dust and fumes. The tiny bunker rooms were more crowded than ever, mostly with persons engaged in caring for and protecting Hitler, or in maintaining his contact with the outside. Of the top Nazi heirarchy only Goebbels and Bormann stayed, Goebbels out of loyalty to the Führer and because he had a vague faith in the miracle, Bormann to promote his own interests and do what damage he could to his rivals. The parade of generals had ended.

Until the 27th Hitler continued to hold the regular situation conferences. Although he attempted still to maintain the tone of a strategist, his span of practical concern had narrowed to such decisions as the appointment of a detachment that was to act (to rescue or kill him) 'in case a Russian tank by some sly trick or other digs me out of here'. A recurring theme in his rambling discourses was the correctness of his decision to stay in Berlin – as an object lesson to all the generals who had ordered retreats and as the only means of achieving a 'moral' victory that would convince the British and Americans of his value to them in their, in his opinion, forthcoming conflict with the Soviet Union.

On the night of the 28th Weidling brought a breakout plan to Hitler. The Führer listened with some interest, but then declared it was better he stay where he was, otherwise he would have to await the end 'somewhere under the open sky or in a farmhouse'. Hitler had made his last military decision. At midnight Dönitz's liaison officer in the bunker radioed, 'We will hold out to the end'.

Greim and Hanna Reitsch flew out that night in an old Arado trainer a Luftwaffe pilot managed somehow to land and get off the ground again. Greim had orders to organise air support for Wenck's attack, and he had a special mission from Hitler – to arrest Himmler for treason. In the evening news had reached the bunker of Himmler's attempt to negotiate an armistice

The Führer inspects damage to the Reich Chancellory

through Count Bernadotte. Hitler had long considered most, if not all, of the generals to be traitors, but he seems actually to have believed that his old Party stalwarts would follow him to the end. In the early morning, he had Bormann dispatch the following radio message to Dönitz: 'The foreign press reports fresh treason. The Führer expects that you will act with lightning speed and iron severity against all traitors in the north German area. Without exception, Schörner, Wenck, and the others must give evidence of their loyalty by the quickest relief of the Führer'.

At daylight Wenck's XX Corps attacked with the 'Clausewitz', 'Scharnhorst', and 'Theodor Körner' Divisions, all so-called youth divisions made up of men from the officer training schools. They added a last flash of the old German *élan* to an otherwise dismal scene and by afternoon had covered fifteen miles to the tip of Lake Schwielow south-west of Potsdam; but their flanks were open and the Lehnin Forest behind them was filled with Russians who rapidly recovered from the initial surprise and shock. To continue the advance all the way to

Berlin, still twenty miles away, was clearly out of the question. After dark the Potsdam garrison made contact and began coming out by rowboat across the lake. Later in the night Keitel authorised Wenck to stop the attack, 'If the Commanding General, XII Army, in full knowledge of his present situation at XX Corps and despite the high historical and moral responsibility that he carries considers continuing the attack toward Berlin not executable . . .'

Through the better part of that day, 29th April, Army Group Vistula was without an effective command. Heinrici refused to order any withdrawals, which meant in effect that he gave no orders at all. He learned during the day that Jodl had intervened in the internal working of the army group to the extent of instructing at least one corps on the south flank to report to him immediately any withdrawal orders coming from the army group. In the morning Manteuffel had declined to take command, stating in his message to Keitel, 'Beg not at this time of crisis in own army to be charged with the mission that the [present] commanding general, who has full confidence of all commanders, is alleged not to have carried out'. The army commanders Manteuffel and

119

Tippelskirch, whose Headquarters, XXI Army, was then taking over the south front from Steiner, had agreed beforehand not to let the command be taken out of Heinrici's hands.

In the afternoon, Keitel and Jodl, knowing that Tippelskirch also intended to refuse, went to Tippelskirch's command post and in an hourlong interview prevailed on him to take acting command until Colonel-General Kurt Student could arrive from Holland. Keitel 'reminded Tippelskirch of his duty most forcefully'. Tippelskirch, although he, like most German generals, found it virtually impossible to refuse a direct order, was no coward and had shown independence of judgment before, notably as Commanding General, IV Army, during the 1944 collapse of Army Group Centre. Apparently what convinced him to desert Heinrici was Jodl's argument that the army group had to hold as much territory as it still could, not for the sake of relieving Berlin, but to give the political authorities something with which to bargain.

During the day, 2nd Belorussian Front's offensive carried past Anklam on the north, past Neubrandenburg and Neustrelitz in the centre and across the Havel in the Zehdenick Liebenwalde sector in the South. Behind Army Group Vistula, Montgomery that day took a bridgehead across the Elbe at Lauenburg upstream from Hamburg. Dönitz, worried by the threat of a thrust from Lauenburg toward Hamburg and Lübeck, which would cut off his headquarters in Jutland, asked that the reinforcements for Army Group Vistula and XII Army be committed on the Elbe instead. Shortly after noon, the balloon being used to beam voice transmissions into Berlin was shot down. Since its headquarters was then practically in the front, the Armed Forces High Command began moving north from Neu Roofen several hours later.

In the *Fuhrerbunker* the 19th was a day of waiting while, above ground, destruction rained down on all sides. Hitler had married Eva Braun the night before and in the early morning hours had written his personal and political testaments. In the latter he named Dönitz his successor as head of state and authorised him to assume the title President of the Reich. Hitler had taken the powers of the president after Hindenburg's death in 1934, but had never himself used the title. Dictator to the last, he appointed a cabinet to take office under Dönitz with Goebbels as Chancellor and Bormann as Party Minister. He knew almost to the hour how much time he had left. Weidling had reported that planes had dropped only a few tons of supplies during the night; in the coming night he expected none at all; mostly likely, the ammunition would run out by nightfall on the 30th.

Hitler dispatched his last message shortly before midnight on the 29th. In five short questions addressed to Jodl he reached for the miracle one more time:

1. Where are Wenck's spearheads?
2. When will they attack again?
3. Where is the IX Army?
4. To where is it breaking through?
5. Where are Holste's XXXXI Panzer Corps spearheads?

There would be no miracle; the Führer had to be told; and Keitel, conscious of history, took the responsibility. In the dry, impersonal language of a situation report he put a period to one of the greatest and most disastrous military adventures the world had ever seen:

To 1. Wenck's point is stopped south of Schwielow Lake. Strong Soviet attacks on the whole east flank.

To 2. As a consequence Twelfth Army cannot continue the attack toward Berlin.

To 3 and 4. IX Army is encircled. A Panzer group has broken out to the west. Location unknown.

To 5. Corps Holste is forced to the defensive from Brandenburg via Rathenow to Kremmen.

The attack toward Berlin has not progressed at any point since Army Group Vistula was also forced to the defensive on its whole front from north of Oranienburg via Neu Brandenburg to Anklam.

Overleaf: Homeless now, former occupants have scrawled messages round the door of a bombed out house. *Right :* Those who tried to desert were shot

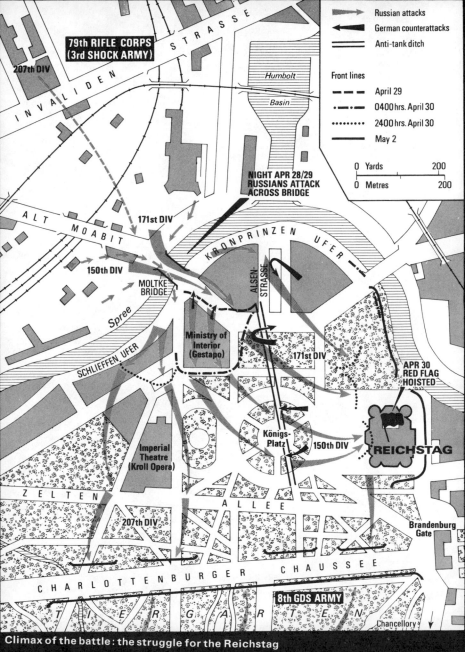

Russian attacks

German counterattacks

Anti-tank ditch

Front lines

- – – April 29
- ·–·–· 0400 hrs. April 30
- ········ 2400 hrs. April 30
- ──── May 2

0 Yards 200

0 Metres 200

79th RIFLE CORPS (3rd SHOCK ARMY)

INVALIDEN STRASSE

207th DIV

Humbolt

Basin

ALT MOABIT

171st DIV

NIGHT APR 28/29 RUSSIANS ATTACK ACROSS BRIDGE

KRONPRINZEN UFER

150th DIV

MOLTKE BRIDGE

ALSEN-STRASSE

Spree

SCHLIEFFEN UFER

Ministry of Interior (Gestapo)

171st DIV

APR 30 RED FLAG HOISTED

Imperial Theatre (Kroll Opera)

Königs-Platz

150th DIV

REICHSTAG

ZELTEN

ALLEE

Brandenburg Gate

207th DIV

CHARLOTTENBURGER CHAUSSEE

8th GDS ARMY

T   I   E   R   G   A   R   T   E   N

Chancellory

Climax of the battle: the struggle for the Reichstag

Breidenstein
Bln-Schöneberg
Kufsteinerstr. 12
Vietheer
Augsburgerstr.
73 I
Bayreuter
Rehberg
Bunker!
Fam. Stolz
Nachr. Ers. Abt. 3
Potsdam
2 Gens. Kp.
Familie
Vogel und
Breidenstein
Schöneberg, Kufsteiner Straße 12
Vietheer: leben alle
ebenso: Dümpelman

On the afternoon of the 30th at about half past three, Hitler and his wife committed suicide. Hitler shot himself through the head, and Eva Hitler took poison. The SS guards carried the bodies outside, tried to burn them in gasoline, and when that failed and the gasoline ran out, buried the remains in a nearby shell hole. A quarter mile away the Russians were storming the Reichstag. Bormann sent a radio-message to Dönitz telling him that he was appointed Hitler's successor and was 'empowered immediately to take all of the measures required by the current situation'. Bormann, however, did not include the most vital piece of information, namely, that the Führer was dead. That was a trump he was not ready to let out of his hand.

At exactly the time the SS men were disposing of Hitler's body behind the pile of rubble that had been the Reich Chancellery, Keitel transmitted a directive to Winter at Command Staff B. The first sentence read: 'The attempt to relieve Berlin has failed'. In the north, Keitel continued, the intention was to have XII Army fight its way north to Army Group Vistula and thereafter, with the combined forces, to hold a line from the mouth of the Elbe to Havelberg (at the confluence of the Havel and the Elbe) and thence north to Rostock. The mission for the south was to form a 'great ring' with the main effort in the east 'to preserve as much territory as possible from Bolshevism'. 'The battle to win

political time', the directive concluded, 'must be continued'. Every attempt at military or political dissolution must be put down with ruthless force'. Keitel did not know that Hitler was dead, and he was fighting the war the way he knew the Führer expected him to, down even to the attempt to make an outrageous proposal sound plausible by suggesting a 'political' motive.

Those who were left in the *Fuhrerbunker* that night still held three assets, ones they hoped to use to their own advantage: the knowledge that the Führer was dead, the seat of the government (what was left of it), and what could have been the two most powerful offices in the successor government. Like all of the top Nazis, except Hitler, they apparently had no understanding of the world's opinion of them.

Krebs had been a military attaché in Moscow before the war, and he spoke Russian. An hour after midnight on the morning of 1st May, he went through the lines behind a white flag. It was not a long trip. The front was then in the *Tiergarten*, directly adjacent to the Reich Chancellery on the west, and almost up to the *Wilhelmplatz* on the east. Krebs was taken to the 8th Guards Army's forward command post where General Vasili I. Chuikov, who in 1942 had commanded the army that defended Stalingrad, heard his proposal. The Russians were clearly disappointed to learn that Krebs had not come to negotiate a general surrender. He had, in fact, come only to make a deal. He

Russian officer briefs his men in front of of the Reichstag

Hordes of prisoners with their Russian captors

brought, as he put it, for Stalin's exclusive information, the news of Hitler's death, and he proposed that the Russians grant an armistice and allow the successor government to assemble in Berlin. Chuikov telephoned a report to 1st Belorussian Front Headquarters and apparently tried to persuade Krebs to get on to the business of a surrender, which Krebs must have known neither he nor his partners in the *Fuhrerbunker* had the authority to do. Later Sokolovsky, who had in the meantime talked to Moscow, arrived to interview Krebs and give him his answer.

At ten o'clock in the morning, possibly because it appeared that Krebs had not got through, Bormann sent a second radio message to Dönitz. Laconic as the first, it stated only that the testament was in force. Bormann said he would come to Plön; and he advised not making the information public until he arrived. At noon Krebs returned. The Russians would agree to let Dönitz come to Berlin and assemble the government there, but they demanded capitulation and would not grant an armistice. Goebbels insisted that in accordance with Hitler's wishes there be no capitulation and reiterated his already announced intention to share the Führer's fate.

In the afternoon, just twenty nine hours after the event, a message signed by Bormann and Goebbels informed Dönitz that the Führer was dead and named the major appointments Hitler had made in addition to Dönitz's own. (Three couriers carrying copies of the testament for Dönitz and for Schörner

– whom Hitler had appointed his successor as Commander in Chief, Army – had left the *Fuhrerbunker* on the 29th. Although all of them escaped from Berlin, none reached his destination.) Goebbels and his wife committed suicide after killing their children. Bormann probably was killed trying to make his way out of Berlin to claim his post in Dönitz's cabinet, but his death was considered sufficiently uncertain by the International Military Tribunal at Nuremberg to warrant his being tried and condemned *in absentia*. Krebs and Colonel-General Wilhelm Burgdorf, Hitler's infamous chief adjutant and Army officer personnel chief, declared that they would commit suicide and probably did.

The Russian thrusts into Berlin had been stronger from the north and south than from the east and west; consequently, on 1st May, although the pocket was nowhere more than a half mile wide, it still reached almost to the S-Bahn ring on the west and northeast. The Reichstag surrendered on the morning of the 1st. The SS had defended the ruin almost as if it were the symbol of Nazism the Russians took it to be.

The 'Müncheberg' Division – what was left of it: five tanks, four artillery pieces, and a handful of troops – was fighting in the *Tiergarten*, around the aquarium and the *Zoobunker*, the big air raid shelter in the *Tiergarten* inside of which thousands of civilians were by then on the verge of suffocating. The radio operators had their sets turned on but receiving nothing, no reports, and no orders. The Russians were moving through the subway tunnels, their movement betrayed by the cries of the civilians in their path. The smell of decaying flesh was every-

Some refused to flee

where. Rumours of Hitler's death raised talk of a breakout to the west, and shortly before dark a patrol returned with the report that the Havel crossings at Spandau were only lightly guarded.

Shortly after five o'clock on the morning of 2nd May, Chuikov received his second German visitor. It was General Weidling, coming to surrender the city. Weidling had considered a breakout but had decided he had neither the room nor the means to organise it. The negotiations were short. Weidling had nothing with which to bargain. He wrote a proclamation calling on the German troops to surrender; then he made a tape of it to be broadcast by Soviet sound trucks.

In the afternoon Soviet leaflets bearing Weidling's proclamation were dropped in the *Tiergarten* while loudspeakers, tuned up to carry through the noise of battle, made his voice unidentifiable. The battle was over in any case, and the 'Müncheberg' Division with a part of the XVIII Panzer Grenadier Division that turned up at the last minute decided to try to escape to the west. They moved out after dark and at dawn managed to seize a bridge on the Havel, but the Russians kept the bridge under fire from a nearby fort, and hundreds of civilian refugees also trying to escape the doomed city streamed onto the bridge. Finally, the division's tanks and trucks, the few that remained, simply rolled up onto the bridge through and over the mass of refugees. When the infantry crossed the pavement was thick with blood. Having crossed the river, the division began to come apart. Everybody thought only of escape. The rearguards would not hold. In another day, with the burning city still in sight behind them, all that were left were isolated groups, not soldiers any more, merely fugitives hiding where they could in woods and swamps.

The Russian writer Simonov came into the city just after the fighting ended. He says it was 2nd May, but it must have been two or three days later. He walked through the zoo in the *Tiergarten*. The dead Russians were laid on the benches and covered, and the Germans remained where they had fallen. A dead hippopotamus floated in a pond, the fins of an unexploded mortar shell protruding from its side. An old keeper grieved for his dead animals but paid no attention to the dead men scattered about outside the cages. At the Reich Chancellory, soldiers were searching the ruins. They had found Goebbels' corpse, but not yet Hitler's; and Russian troops and vehicles were pouring into the city from all directions.

Surrender

The victors: Marshal Zhukov and his staff at the Brandenburg Gate

Dönitz, on 1st May before he knew Hitler was dead, had pledged 'immutable loyalty' to the Führer and 'to conduct this war to its end in the manner the unique, heroic struggle of the German people demands'. But Dönitz's loyalty was professional, not sentimental. The next day he determined that the German military situation was hopeless, a conclusion he seems successfully to have avoided until then. In directives issued during the day he established as his policy to continue the war against the Soviet Union for the purpose of keeping as many Germans as possible from falling into Soviet hands and to resist the Americans and British only to the extent that they interfered with the attainment of the first objective. He decided to attempt evasion of the unconditional surrender by negotiating piecemeal surrenders 'at the army group level'. As a first step he appointed Admiral Hans-Georg von Friedeburg head of a delegation to negotiate

an agreement with Montgomery to spare Hamburg and 'to discuss farther-reaching questions'.

For Army Group Vistula the end came more quickly and more mercifully than the Germans could have expected. Montgomery's 21st Army Group, after breaking out of its Elbe river bridgehead the day before, on 2nd May, reached the Baltic coast at Wismar and Lübeck. Elements of the United States 9th Army pushed east to Ludwigslust and Schwerin. In Schwerin, American armoured troops captured the Army Group Vistula quartermaster section. General Student, who had taken command of the army group on the 1st, escaped just ahead of the American tanks. The 2nd Belorussian Front reached Wittenberge, Parchim, and Bad Doberan. Between the Soviet and the Anglo-American fronts the III Panzer and XXI Armies were then squeezed into a corridor fifteen to twenty miles wide, stretching from the Elbe river to the coast. During the night on the 2nd Manteuffel and Tippelskirch surrendered their armies, which by then had

The vanquished: Field-Marshal von Rundstedt, with his son (centre) falls into United States Army hands

almost completely disintegrated, to the Americans. Jodl, at the last minute, had drafted an order authorising such a move, but it went into the files with the notation: 'Could no longer be transmitted'.

The XII Army's XX Corps had begun falling back south-west of Potsdam during the night of 1st May. The next morning it took through its line 30,000 IX Army survivors with whom it had established radio contact and thus guided to its front and away from the strongest Russian concentrations. On the afternoon of the 3rd, Wenck sent General Maximilian Freiherr von Edelsheim across the Elbe to the United States 9th Army to negotiate a surrender. General Simpson consented to let as many of the German IX and XII Armies' troops cross the Elbe as could without (except for the wounded) assistance from the Americans. Between the morning of the 5th and the night of the 7th most of Wenck's force took refuge behind the American line. The Germans found it incomprehensible that the Americans refused also to receive through their line the many thousands of German civilian refugees who crowded up to the east bank of the Elbe and subsequently fell into the hands of the Russians.

Army Groups Centre and Courland and the Army of East Prussia, those sad monuments to Hitler's strategy, posed greater problems. Dönitz's first impulse had been to order Army Group Centre to start retreating westward at once; but he had been dissuaded by Keitel who, drawing the wrong conclusions to the last, had argued that if the army group left its built-up line, it would not be able to preserve a solid front. To Army Group Courland and Army of East Prussia, Dönitz sent word that he proposed to secure British and American toleration of, and 'under certain circumstances support for', an evacuation that would return to Germany 50,000 men from Army Group Courland and as many as 100,000 from Army of East

The fit had to march

Prussia 'in the first ten days'. On 4th May when Friedeburg reported that Montgomery had agreed to accept the surrender of all the German forces in Holland, Denmark, and north Germany, Dönitz instructed him to contact Eisenhower and negotiate another partial capitalution. He was 'above all to explain to Eisenhower why a total capitalution on all fronts appears impossible to the Grand-Admiral'. On the 6th Friedeburg reported that Eisenhower demanded an immediate and simultaneous unconditional surrender.

That afternoon Jodl arrived at the SHAEF forward headquarters in Reims. Dönitz had sent him with instructions to lay before Eisenhower again 'completely and openly' the reasons why the Germans considered a total capitulation impossible. Failing of success in that, he was to try to get a phased capitulation with as long an interval as possible between the time the fighting terminated and the time the troops had to surrender their arms and cease all movements. Fifteen minutes after midnight, Dönitz received a radio message from

Jodl stating that Eisenhower insisted that the total capitulation be signed 'today' to take effect at midnight on the night of the 8th; otherwise he would close the front to all Germans, including troops coming from the east. Jodl added, 'I see no way out but to sign'.

Dönitz concluded that Jodl, who before his departure had been the one who argued most strongly against total capitulation, must have been convinced that no better terms could be obtained. He, therefore, empowered Jodl to sign, and at a quarter to one in the morning the new Foreign Minister, Graf Lutz Schwerin von Krosigk, announced the surrender over the German radio. At half past one Dönitz ordered all the commanders on the Eastern Front to take their troops west as fast as they could and to 'fight their way through the Russians' if they had to; all hostilities against the Western Allies were to cease at once. At a quarter to two, in the SHAEF war room in Reims, Jodl placed his signature on the Act of Military Surrender. Lieutenant-General Walter Bedell Smith, the SHAEF Chief of Staff, signed for the

Supreme Commander; and Major-General Ivan Suslaparov signed on behalf of the Soviet Supreme Command. The time for all German forces to cease active operations and 'to remain in the positions occupied at that time' was sent at one minute after eleven o'clock on the night of 8th May.

The Act of Military Surrender was a short document, five paragraphs in all; and it simply stated that the German High Command surrendered unconditionally to the SupremeCommander, Allied Expeditionary Force, and simultaneously to the Soviet Supreme Command all the German forces on land, sea and air. The document had been drafted at the last minute at SHAEF headquarters. The EAC surrender instrument, the result of half a year's negotiations, was not used. To the huge embarrassment of the Americans especially, it was discovered later that the approved EAC surrender instrument had never been transmitted to Eisenhower through his command channel, the Combined Chiefs-of-Staff.

Although the signing at Reims was completely adequate to accomplish the German surrender, the Russians insisted on a second full-dress signing in Berlin. Eisenhower, as the senior commander of the Western Allies, took the stand that the surrender had been accomplished at Reims and the Berlin ceremony was only a ratification. He, therefore, did not attend in person, but sent his deputy Air Chief-Marshal Tedder at the head of a delegation that included General Carl Spaatz, commander of the United States strategic air force in Europe, and General Jean de Lattre de Tassigny, commander of the French 1st Army.

The ceremony was scheduled for two o'clock on the afternoon of the 8th. The SHAEF representative arrived on time, but had to wait several hours for the arrival from Moscow of Zhukov's political advisor, Andrey Y. Vishinsky. By then a second hitch had already developed. The Russians had decorated one wall of the room in which the signing was to take place, a small dining hall in the Karlshorts Military En-

The wounded wait for transport

gineering College in the south-eastern suburbs of Berlin, with the flags of the victors. The flag of France was missing, and de Lattre protested. The Russians, not having a French flag, agreed to make one; but on the first attempt they came up with the Dutch flag.

After Vishinsky, whom the visitors knew by reputation as the prosecutor at the Soviet purge trials of the 1930's, arrived it appeared for some hours that the signing might not take place at all, at least not in time to have any significance. Zhukov and Tedder had agreed to sign as principals with Spaatz and de Lattre as witnesses, which would have followed a precedent set at Reims where the French Major-General François Sevez had signed as a witness. Vishinsky declared that de Lattre might sign to symbolise the revival of France, but that Tedder represented both the British and the United States forces and, therefore, Spaatz could not sign. Spaatz insisted on signing if de Lattre did, and the French general declared that he would deserve to be hanged if he returned to France without having put his name on the German capitulation. It was close to eleven o'clock at night before the Russians agreed to let both sign – somewhat below the signatures of the principals.

The ceremony began shortly after eleven and might at times have appeared almost comic had the occa-sion been a less somber one. The room was too small to hold comfortably all the officers and newspaper correspondents. Tedder had brought three plane-loads of people with him. Three Soviet generals who arrived late took seats at a small table with three empty chairs – the table reserved for the German delegation – and had to be shooed off. De Lattre impressed the Russians most, mainly because of the cut of his uniform. Spaatz, to them, looked irritated and uncomfortable, which he no doubt was. After the Soviet and Western representatives were seated, Zhukov gave orders to admit the German delegation, Keitel, Friedeburg, Colonel-General Hans Jürgen Stumpff, representing the Luftwaffe, and a half dozen aides. Keitel, wearing a monocle, aroused annoyance with his arrogant demeanor and nonplussed many of those present when he saluted with his marshal's baton, a gesture which looked as if he were doing an exercise with a dumb-bell. The rest of the Germans were grave, apparently, barely able to keep their composure. The signing was completed at about fifteen minutes before midnight. The Germans were the last to sign. After he dismissed the Germans, Zhukov offered souvenir pens to those present in the room, but nobody took any. All of the signatories had used their own pens – except Spaatz and de Lattre who, after arguing long for their right to sign, discovered they had not brought pens.

Having signed the surrender, Dönitz and the Armed Forces High Command

Russian victory

were not sure they could enforce it on the Eastern Front. Their uncertainty was undoubtedly inspired in part by a desire to see the terms concerning surrender to the Russians evaded to the greatest extent possible without incurring reprisals. Jodl had taken out some advance insurance by securing a statement from Eisenhower's chief of staff, Smith, that the Armed Forces High Command would not be held responsible if 'individual soldiers and some troops units' did not follow orders and refused to surrender to the Russians.

The source of most concern was Army Group Centre, because it was the largest single force still on the Eastern Front, because it had the farthest to go to reach the lines of the Western Allies (of those that had any chance of doing so at all), and because no one knew how Schörner would react to the surrender. Schörner had reported on 2nd May that he had a tight hold on his troops and was starting to manufacture his own ammunition and motor fuel. The last heard from him was that he intended to fight his way through to the line of the Elbe and Vltava (Moldau) before surrendering. On the 8th a colonel on the Armed Forces High Command staff went to Schörner's headquarters with an American officer escort. The colonel reported that Schörner had ordered the surrender terms observed but claimed he did not have the means to make certain they were carried out everywhere. The colonel 'assured him that the command difficulties would be brought to the attention of the Armed Forces High Command and the Americans'. Dönitz need neither have worried about Schörner's attempting a last-ditch battle nor have hoped that he would find a means to extricate his army group. Schörner deserted his troops on the 8th when in civilian clothes he flew a light plane out of Czechoslovakia. He was arrested ten days later in Austria by German troops and turned over to the Americans.

53 miles – 55 days

The war was over, but the Russians gave no sign of wanting to share Berlin. In fact, the original reason for the Western Allies being in a hurry to get to Berlin – to take charge of the German central administration – practically no longer existed. The German government had collapsed even more completely than had been expected, and of what remained of it very little was in Berlin. The SHAEF forces had captured the German northern and southern command staffs, and eventually they uncovered in the western zones what were probably greater portions of the German records and ministry personnel than those falling to the Russians.

In the northern command staff SHAEF had possession of both the Armed Forces High Command and the successor German government to the extent that one existed. After the surrender was signed, neither was of much use. Both were willing, even eager, to function as policy-making bodies, but they had no organizations through which to function, and the Allies were determined to do the policy making themselves. Dönitz had moved his headquarters to Flensburg just south of the Danish border, and there a SHAEF Ministerial Control Party took him and his associates under surveillance after the surrender. SHAEF refused to recognise his group as constituting anything more than a remnant of the Armed Forces High Command, but Dönitz had been careful to authenticate his appointment as Hitler's successor and thus posed a potential legal problem for the occupation. On the other hand, Dönitz and nearly all of his immediate subordinates were in the Allied automatic arrest categories, either as war criminals or as dangerous Nazis, and on the morning of 23rd May Eisenhower resolved the question of their future by having them all placed under arrest.

But although controlling the German government no longer was important, the establishment of four power control of Germany had acquired a burning urgency for the British and Americans, and Berlin was to be the seat of the Allied Control Authority. The Russians, however, seemed not to share the Western Powers' concern; and, to the British and Americans' considerable chagrin, the planned four power control encountered a legal obstacle after the surrender. The Act of Military Surrender had accomplished the capitulation of the German Armed Forces, but it contained no reference to the Allied intention to assume supreme political authority in Germany. Further, it could potentially be construed as not affecting the civil government of Germany at all. After 9th May, therefore, the EAC had to set to work once more to devise a document that would remedy those omissions and establish a legal basis for Allied Control.

For the time being, the Russians were perfectly content to have Berlin to themselves. Zhukov had appointed Colonel-General N. Z. Berzarin city commandant on 28th April, and while rape and looting did not stop at once, Berzarin did succeed in restoring a considerable amount of order after the surrender. On 30th April, Walter Ulbricht had left Moscow with a plane-load of German emigré Communists. Two days later, before the fighting ceased, they were in Berlin, selecting Germans to form a city government. In the succeeding weeks they worked at top speed to establish administrations in all the boroughs, including those to be occupied by the Western Allies, appointing so-called 'bourgeois' anti-Fascists' to the majority of posts but always reserving the crucial positions for Communists. Also early on the scene were the Soviet reparations teams. Using requisitioned German labour, they dismantled for shipment to Russia the factories that had survived the bombing and shelling, especially those in the future sectors of the Western Allies.

Once the fighting was over, the Russians apparently developed a certain pride in and affection for Berlin. For one thing, they seem rapidly to have convinced themselves that the battle had been brilliantly fought and somehow had been decisive in the war. For another, they obviously believed that Berlin was the true heart of Germany and that to have Berlin amounted to possessing a kind of psychological hold on the rest of the country – and they were perhaps not entirely mistaken. Berzarin, in what was then

But there was still the need for vigilance

entirely untypical behavior for a
Russian, sometimes talked and acted
as if he were running for public office,
and the Russians never failed to point
out to the few newspaper correspondents allowed into the city that Berlin
was theirs by right of conquest and
that the Western Allies desire also to
be there was almost parasitic. Of
course, they did not mention that they
would get in exchange a full third of
their occupation zone, including Leipzig, the largest city wholly within the
zone, to which the Western forces also
could lay claim by right of conquest.

For SHAEF and the west Germans in
the months of May and June 1945
Berlin was only a voice, albeit a per-
sistent one. The Russians began
operating Radio Berlin soon after the
surrender on a 19 hour a day schedule.
While SHAEF-operated Radio Luxembourg in its daily four hours of German
broadcasting kept its listeners on a
dour fare consisting mostly of military
government announcements and accounts of German atrocities, Radio
Berlin regaled the Germans with
music, friendly chats, announcements
of cinemas and theaters reopening in
Berlin, and accounts of rapid recon-
struction allegedly being accomplished in Berlin and the Soviet zone. With
programmes such as one entitled
'With a Gay Heart the Day Let's
Start', Radio Berlin radiated warmth
to a rejected people. No doubt the
effect was greater outside Berlin and
outside the Soviet-held areas.

At the end of May the EAC completed
and the governments approved a
'Declaration Regarding the Defeat of
Germany and the Assumption of
Supreme Authority by the Allied
Powers'. In part it read like another
surrender document, even to ordering
all German forces to cease hostilities
immediately. Probably no nation in
history has been required to surrender
so completely, so abjectly, or so often.
The Declaration did, however, close
the potential loopholes left by the Act
of Military Surrender. The formal
signing was delegated to the four
Allied commanders in chief in Germany, and to the Western Allies,
at least, the occasion also seemed an
appropriate one for establishing the
Allied Control Authority, presumably
with its seat in Berlin.

On 5th June, Eisenhower, Montgomery, and de Lattre went to Berlin,
that is, they went to Wendenschloss, a
suburban community formerly in-
habited by wealthy Germans and Nazi
big-shots which the Russians had

Conquering generals, left to right,
Montgomery, Eisenhower, Zhukov and
de Lattre de Tassigny

tightly cordoned off from the rest of
the city. The generals' instructions
were to sign the Declaration and
propose that the Allied Control Council therewith be considered established, the signing ceremony being its
first session. They were aware that an
entirely different question, namely,
when the SHAEF would evacuate the
territory of the Soviet zone it held,
might be uppermost in the Russians'
minds, but they were hoping they
would not have to answer it just then
since the British and United States
Governments had not yet agreed on
what to do. Churchill was urging that
the Western Allies retain the Soviet
territory until the Russians made
suitable commitments on the administration of Germany. The United
States Government was unwilling to
bargain so baldly, but apparently had
not decided what other course it would
take. Consequently, the generals'
orders were to insist that the establishment of the Control Council was
not contingent on a withdrawal from
the Soviet Zone, and they were to

make no commitments regarding a
withdrawal.

The signing was held in the yacht
club at Wendenschloss not far from a
large lake-side villa the Russians had
requisitioned as Zhukov's residence.
At the conclusion, Eisenhower proposed that the work of the Control
Council be begun. He and Montgomery
had each brought a half dozen plane-
loads of officers with them, obviously
intending to leave many of them behind to launch the administration in
Berlin. Zhukov flatly refused to have
the Control Council set up before the
troops were in their assigned zones.
He said he could not participate in
deciding questions relating to Germany as a whole when he did not have
all of his zone. He also refused to consider permitting any of the subordinate agencies to begin work. When
Montgomery interposed that it would
take time to redeploy the British
and United States troops, Zhukov
asked, 'How long?' Montgomery said
about three weeks. Zhukov declared

Right: Allies for the moment, British,
American, and Russian soldiers show
what they think of the Führer

138

that was fine; it would give the commanders time to gather their Control Council staffs.

Eisenhower and Montgomery returned to their headquarters in the west the same afternoon. The Russians had prepared an elaborate banquet but showed no desire to accommodate even overnight the retinues the generals had brought along; so the planes had to be flown back in time to land in daylight. The question of establishing the Control Council and with it that of the Western Allies' entry into Berlin went back to the governments. If anything, Berlin appeared more inaccessible than before; the western representatives had been unable to detect any signs of Soviet readiness to

The cold in the streets

establish four power control.

Meanwhile, the time before the Big Three meeting at Potsdam, scheduled for mid-July, was growing short. Under that pressure, Churchill gave up his insistence on holding part of the Soviet zone. He found the alternative – having to go to Berlin on the sufferance of the Russians and without a sector of his own – too uncomfortable. President Harry S Truman, in a letter to Stalin, thereupon proposed that the Western Allies' withdrawal from the Soviet zone and their entry into Berlin be accomplished simultaneously. The Western Allies, he added, would require transit rights across the Soviet zone from their zones to Berlin. Stalin agreed and proposed to have the movements start on 1st July and be completed on 4th July. Zhukov,

The Big Three; Churchill, Truman and Stalin at Potsdam

he said, had full authority to arrange the transit rights.

In late June, the Americans decided to have a preliminary look at their Berlin sector. The Russians had agreed to let a convoy through to Babelsberg, the former German film colony outside Potsdam which was to be used to billet the United States delegation to the Big Three conference in July. The convoy as it was finally made up numbered some one hundred vehicles and five hundred officers and men, about half of them military government personnel under Colonel Frank L Howley, the commanding officer of Military Government Detachment A1A1, the Berlin detachment. Portentiously designated the Preliminary Reconnaissance Party, Berlin, the convoy set out on 23rd June and was promptly stopped as it attempted to cross into Soviet territory via the Elbe bridge at Dessau. After seven hours of arguing with a succession of Soviet generals, the Americans got fifty vehicles, thirty seven officers, and one hundred and

seventy five men across, exactly the number the Russians had agreed to pass in the first place. Of the military government contingent only Howley and three other officers got through.

For the Americans the fifty mile trip was instructive. They saw Soviet displaced persons, who a day or two before had crossed the Elbe from the west in a holiday mood, trudging tiredly along the road toward Berlin. The Soviet horse-drawn supply trains struck them as being more appropriate to the American Civil War than to the Second World War, and the Soviet soldiers they saw looked dirty and indifferent. The opportunities for observation ended at Babelsberg. There Russian guards refused to let anyone leave the American compound, and Howley returned to his detachment more than half convinced it would never see service in Berlin.

The talk was that it would be easier for the Western Allies to fight their way to Berlin than to get there by agreement with the Russians, and nobody imagined then what was still to come. On the 29th Lieutenant-General Lucius du B Clay and Lieutenant-General Sir Ronald Weeks, the

Berlin under occupation; a Russian policewoman directs traffic

American and British Deputy Military Governors, went to Berlin to discuss the transit arrangements Stalin had said Zhukov was empowered to make. The Russians who on the two previous occasions had displayed particular friendliness toward de Lattre, this time refused to admit a French representative because France did not yet have a sector assigned in Berlin. Clay and Weeks asked for general access by air and over the main highways and railroads running from their zones to Berlin. Zhukov would only agree to two air corridors, two raillines, and one highway. As a conces-sion, he said the Americans might use the Halle Dessau Berlin highway, of which the Halle Dessau stretch was then still in American hands, until 7th July when it would be closed because of the Potsdam Conference. Since the time was too short to carry the argu-ment back through governmental channels, Clay and Weeks accepted under protest. Zhukov had one other point to make: he did not want any kind of formal turnover of the Soviet zone territory the SHAEF forces would evacuate. In fact, he wanted a interval of two to three miles between the Soviet advance guards and the SHAEF rear guards, enough pretty well to keep the main forces out of sight of each other.

Divided city

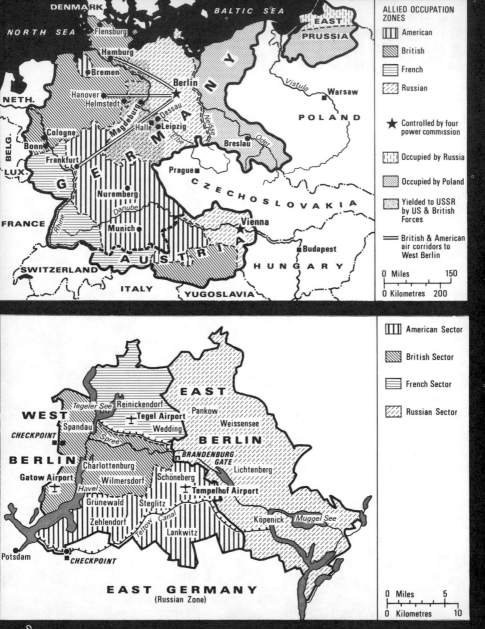

ALLIED OCCUPATION ZONES

▥	American
▧	British
▤	French
▨	Russian

★ Controlled by four power commission

▦ Occupied by Russia

▩ Occupied by Poland

▨ Yielded to USSR by US & British Forces

═ British & American air corridors to West Berlin

0 Miles 150
0 Kilometres 200

DENMARK
BALTIC SEA
EAST PRUSSIA
NORTH SEA
Flensburg
Hamburg
Bremen
Berlin ★
Vistula
Warsaw
POLAND
NETH.
Hanover
Helmstedt
Magdeburg
Halle
Dessau
Leipzig
BELG.
Cologne
Bonn
Frankfurt
Elbe
Neisse
Oder
Breslau
LUX.
G E R M A N Y
Prague
C Z E C H O S L O V A K I A
Nuremberg
Danube
Rhine
Munich
Vienna ★
A U S T R I A
Budapest
H U N G A R Y
FRANCE
SWITZERLAND
ITALY
YUGOSLAVIA

Berlin Sectors

▥	American Sector
▧	British Sector
▤	French Sector
▨	Russian Sector

WEST BERLIN
Tegeler See
Reinickendorf
Tegel Airport
Spandau
Wedding
EAST BERLIN
Pankow
Weissensee
CHECKPOINT
Spree
Charlottenburg
BRANDENBURG GATE
Lichtenberg
Gatow Airport
Havel
Wilmersdorf
Schöneberg
Tempelhof Airport
Grünewald
Steglitz
Zehlendorf
Teltow Canal
Lankwitz
Köpenick
Müggel See
Potsdam
CHECKPOINT

EAST GERMANY
(Russian Zone)

0 Miles 5
0 Kilometres 10

Under Four-Power control: how the Allies divided both country and capital

After the Babelsberg trip Howley looked for a place to settle his detachment – and wait. When he found a spot outside Halle, he proposed to move there on Sunday 1st July. On Saturday he received an order directing him to take the detachment to Berlin, and on Sunday morning, in combat uniform and carrying field packs, the 85 officers and 136 enlisted men of Detachment A1A1 moved out of Halle, passed Dessau, crossed the Elbe, and without any trouble headed for Berlin. By nightfall the detachment had pitched camp and had a hot meal in the Grünewald, the park-like forest on the south-western outskirts of Berlin.

The other British and American parties to start that day were not as fortunate. At Dessau and Magdeburg the local Soviet commanders first denied that they had authority to let the British and Americans pass. Then they became elaborately concerned over the safety of bridges, closing them at random for hours-long inspections and repairs. The Russians refused to let the first British party on the Magdeburg route cross the Elbe on the *Autobahn* bridge at all, and the British finally crossed after several hours' delay on one of the bridges in the city that the Russians were not guarding.

The British and Americans had scheduled their main occupation forces to move on the 3rd and 4th, and both planned impressive entries into Berlin. The American crack 2nd Armoured Division began its march on the morning of the 3rd to be in Berlin in time to stage an Independence Day parade on the 4th. The Russians stopped the division for six hours at Dessau claiming that several bridges were unsafe and then closed the Dessau Berlin road altogether, forcing the division to detour 65 miles to Helmstedt.

In Berlin at noon on the 2nd, Major-General Floyd L Parks and Major-General Lewis O Lyne, the American and British garrison commanders for Berlin, met with Colonel General Aleksandr V Gorbatov, who had replaced Berzarin as Soviet commandant in the city after the latter's death in an automobile accident. They agreed that the Americans and British would assume control of their sectors in Berlin at midnight on the night of the 4th and Gorbatov promised Soviet participation in the formal ceremony of occupation and the parade the Americans were planning.

The parade was held on the afternoon of the 4th in the Adolf Hitler caserne by as much of the 2nd Armoured Division as had made its way into the city. Troops and command alike were tired and thoroughly irritated, and just as the parade ended Parks received a message from Zhukov stating that the western sectors would not be turned over until after the *Kommandatura* had been established to control Berlin as a whole. Parks, his faith in inter-Allied co-operation worn thin, attempted to reach Zhukov and when he failed told Howley to move his detachment into the American boroughs as planned, adding, 'Don't get into too much trouble', The British, meanwhile, were in so much of a tangle as a result of the Russian interference on the access routes that they had refused to take over their sector before Zhukov's message reached them.

The next morning the six American *Verwaltungsbezirk* detachments moved into their assigned boroughs. By nine o'clock they had opened offices, hung out the American flag, and posted the military government ordinances. The Russians were late sleepers, and it was eleven before they came around to protest. The language difference hampered discussion somewhat, but both sides had essentially only one point to make: the Russians that Marshal Zhukov said, 'No', the Americans that General Gorbatov had said 'Yes'. The Russians said they had their orders, and the Americans said they had theirs. In the end the Americans stayed, and the Russians stayed. In a day or two, when the Russians learned they would not be punished for having failed to keep the Americans out, some of them became quite friendly. The Americans, having made their point, did not insist for the time being on taking actual control of the administration.

Berlin was quiet, deathly quiet. In the worst damaged sections block on block of rubble, the remains of buildings pounded almost to dust, stretched for miles. Bomb and shell craters, half

Long after the battle subsided, the search for mines went on

filled with water, pitted the streets. The bridges over the city's many canals had nearly all collapsed under the bombing and artillery fire or been blown by the retreating Germans; and the canals were stagnant and covered with scum, the breeding places of billions of mosquitos and flies. Sewers hung under the bridges had fractured and were pouring their effluent into the canals. The city was literally a huge cemetery. Graves marked by crude wooden crosses without names of other identification were to be seen everywhere, in the public squares and along the streets; and thousands lay unburied under the rubble. Some thirty seven buses, one hundred subway cars, and a few streetcars drawn by steam engines were the only means of transportation. The people were getting 64% of a daily 1,240-calorie ration.

The liveliest activity was to be found in the black markets that by July had become virtually permanent institutions in the Tiergarten and the Alexanderplatz. Many Germans had accumulated large sums of money during the years of wartime austerity, and they willingly paid enormous prices for useful or edible goods. For the Germans, however, money was

ceasing to be a medium of exchange, and most goods were bartered. The arrival of the Americans almost instantly opened a whole new phase in Berlin black-marketeering, a trade in cigarettes, candy bars, other small luxury items that the United States troops had in abundance and the Soviet troops did not have at all, and wrist watches – above all wrist watches.

The Western Allies had, with considerable reluctance, given the Russians duplicate plates for printing Allied Military Marks, the official occupation currency. The marks for the Americans, British, and French were all printed in Washington and controlled. The Russians printed their own in a quantity to suit themselves, and they then paid off their troops to whom in most cases they owed years of back pay. Under the Soviet system the marks were not convertible into roubles; so the soldiers had no choice but to spend or lose them. Consequently, wrist watches in particular – the Russian soldier's idea of the ultimate in elegance – went for as much as a thousand dollars in Allied Military Marks. For the American soldiers the marks were convertible, which meant the thousand dollars was eventually paid by the United States taxpayer.

The boroughs in the United States

Above left: Now Germany feels the despair that Russia knew. *Below:* The job of clearing Berlin begins. *Above:* Old men had to help

sector were typical of the rest of Berlin. Damage ranged from 70% in the outlying districts to above 90% in the city's centre. In the industrial plants 95% of the machines had either been destroyed in the bombing or dismantled and shipped to the Soviet Union. The American military government officers suspected that one reason the Russians were reluctant to relinquish control was that they wanted time to remove the remaining 5%, but it could at least be said that the Russians did not favour any part of the city. They were as busy stripping their own zone as they had been the western zones. They had, nevertheless, made a respectable start on the monumental clean-up job Berlin faced. Their method was simple. Gangs of Germans, mostly women, worked on the mountainous heaps of rubble using some to fill in the craters in the streets and rearranging the rest into less obtrusive patterns. The Americans observed that the Russians showed no concern for efficiency or skill; they merely gave orders and kept the Germans at work until the job was done. To them, quality was unimportant, and in dismantling factories, where the same system was used, much valuable equipment had been ruined before it left the premises.

The Germans were relieved to see the Americans arrive. Although the Soviet Command had not imposed non-fraternisation regulations such as those the Americans and British were still trying to enforce upon themselves, the Russians' official arbitrariness and individual unpredictability had aroused insecurity and fear that persisted even though they also often displayed personal generosity and kindness. Looting and plundering had subsided to sporadic acts by undisciplined and usually drunken individuals, and rape had become an unnecessarily strenuous way of attaining something that in a war-

Women were pressed in gangs to remove the rubble

Left: With starvation all too close, mobile canteens were quickly swamped. *Above:* And the exchange trade was always busy

torn, almost starving city hundreds of women were willing to provide on professional or semi-professional terms.

The great danger was that the city might yet, after having survived the war, succumb to hunger or disease. Refugees and evacuees were coming from all directions, many from as far away as Czechoslovakia, thus increasing the population by thousands each day. They all came on foot with no more possessions than could be pushed in a hand cart, a baby carriage, or on a bicycle. They sought shelter in hastily built camps or with relatives, and they brought with them vermin and disease, especially venereal disease. A violent intestinal ailment the Germans called 'hunger typhoid' swept back and forth across the city, carried probably from ruptured sewers into the water systems. Adults and older children generally did not die from it, but it killed 65% of the newborn babies.

While the American military government officers rather admired the technical aspects of the Soviet administration, they were astounded by the Russians' approach to what most Americans then conceived to be the main purpose of the occupation, namely, the educating of the Germans in democratic processes. The American military government organisation featured as one of its prized elements a system of courts in which the Germans could get fair, if occasionally more elaborate than necessary, hearings. Under the Russians, the borough commandant's word was law, and he was the final judge, even in the passing of death sentences. But what surprised the Americans most was the Russians' method of control. The Nazis had used block leaders. The Russians had improved on that by appointing house leaders, one person in every house who was responsible for the political, social, and economic activity of every person in that house. The house leader distributed the ration cards and handed out work assignments, hence their opportunities for graft, blackmail, and petty tyranny were plentiful.

Generals Clay and Weeks met with Zhukov on 6th July at the Soviet headquarters in Berlin-Pankow to determine procedures for the four-power administration of Berlin. The mood, particularly of the Russians, was not friendly at the start, and it grew downright frigid as the conference progressed. Zhukov and the other Soviet generals with him clearly were

For young and aged, the trucks were all the home they had

End of the Reich. Death on the steps of the Reich Chancellory

PRÄSIDIALKANZLEI
DES FÜHRERS
UND
REICHSKANZLERS

reluctant to give up their exclusive control of the city, and they obviously had instructions not to make commitments that would impair the Soviet hold on the eastern sector. Clay proposed running the city as a single unit through a central administration. Zhukov agreed to a central policy-making body, but insisted that each nation have full and exclusive control in its own sector. To Clay's and Week's huge surprise and dismay, he also told them that since the British

With nowhere to go, a refugee waits for orders from the Allies

and Americans were taking over their sectors they would also have to assume responsibility for providing the populations in them with food and coal. The agricultural collection and distribution systems in Brandenburg and Mecklenburg from which Berlin normally drew its supplies, he blandly explained, had completely broken down; and Upper Silesia, in the past the source of much of the city's coal, was now under Polish administration. The most he would consent to was to keep up appearances by maintaining a single distribution and ration system for the whole city – provided the

A Russian officer shows British soldiers the shallow pit where Hitler's body is said to have burned. In the foreground are the fuel tanks used

Americans and British contributed their quotas. Clay and Weeks, who had come hoping to set precedent for treating Germany as an economic if not a political unit, went home with close to a million and a half more mouths to feed out of the already slim resources of the western zones.

The *Kommandatura*, consisting of Generals Gorbatov, Lyne, and Parks, together with their deputies and with Brigadier General Jeoffrey de Beauchesne representing France – which still did not have a sector assigned – held its first meeting on 11th July. Food and coal were the most urgent items of discussion, as they were to be for many meetings in the future. The Russians would not agree to maintain supplies for the western sectors for more than a few days and then only against assurances of repayment. They now also insisted that the regulations and procedures they had instituted during their period of sole occupation be taken over intact by the *Kommandatura*. The Americans and British agreed, intending to make changes later after they had time to study

conditions in their sectors, but that was to prove extraordinarily difficult since *Kommandatura* decisions had to be unanimous and the Russians thus had the power to veto any future changes.

The Soviet troops and military government officers withdrew from the the western sectors at nine o'clock on the morning of 12th July. The *Kommandatura* was in being and the Western Allies at last had their full shares in the occupation of Berlin. The Russians had observed the letter of the protocols on the occupation signed nearly a year before and that was all. The Control Council began meeting in Berlin in August 1945, but it hardly achieved even the status of a pretence at being a central authority for occupied Germany. In the first years of the occupation some saw the Berlin *Kommandatura* as at least a token of continuing inter-Allied co-operation, but it was a false token. Berlin was divided from the first as Germany was divided. It was as if the drives that had begun in June 1944 in the swamps of Belorussia and on the Normandy beaches had reached an impasse but not ended. The city, symbol of conflict in the Second World War, would remain that for another generation or more.

Bibliography

The Fall of Berlin Chuikov, Vasili I
(New York: Holt, Rinehart, Winston,
1968)
The Last Battle Ryan, Cornelius (New
York: Simon and Schuster, 1966)
The Last 100 Days Toland, John (New
York: Random House, 1966)
The Last Days of Hitler Trevor-Roper,
H R (New York: Macmillan, 1947)
Russia at War, 1941–1945 Werth,
Alexander (New York: E. P. Dutton,
1964)
*Stalingrad to Berlin: The German Defeat
in the East* Ziemke, Earl F (Washington
DC: Government Printing Office 1968)